Simon

T0228831

Island Town

methuen | drama

LONDON • NEW YORK • OXFORD • NEW DELHI • SYDNEY

METHUEN DRAMA
Bloomsbury Publishing Plc
50 Bedford Square. London WC1B 3DP. UK
1385 Broadway, New York, NY 10018, USA

BLOOMSBURY, METHUEN DRAMA and the Methuen Drama logo
are trade marks of Bloomsbury Publishing Plc

First published in Great Britain 2018

Cover design by Toby Way
Photography © Ganesha Lockhart

A catalogue record for this book is available from the British Library.

ISBN: PB: 978-1-3500-9226-6
ePDF: 978-1-3500-9227-3
ePub: 978-1-3500-9228-0

Series: Modern Plays

Typeset by Country Setting, Kingdown, Kent CT14 8ES

A Paines Plough and Theatr Clwyd production

ISLAND TOWN

by Simon Longman

ISLAND TOWN

by Simon Longman

KATE	Katherine Pearce
PETE/DAVE/WILL	Jack Wilkinson
SAM/ALEX/LIV	Charlotte O'Leary

Direction	Stef O'Driscoll
Co-Movement Director	Jennifer Jackson
Co-Movement Director	Simon Carroll-Jones
Lighting	Peter Small
Sound and Composition	Dominic Kennedy
Assistant Director	Balisha Karra
Lighting Programmer	Tom Davis
Line Producer	Sofia Stephanou

Company Stage Manager	Caitlin O'Reilly
Technical Stage Manager	Wesley Hughes
Technical Stage Manager (Edinburgh)	Ben Pavey

SIMON LONGMAN | *Writer*

Simon is a writer from the West Midlands whose play *Gundog* recently premiered at the Royal Court Theatre, directed by Vicky Featherstone, and for which he was awarded the 49th George Devine award for Most Promising Playwright. His plays include: *Rails* (Theatre by the Lake); *White Sky* (Royal Welsh College of Music and Drama, Royal Court); *Spooks* (Old Red Lion) and *Milked* (Pentabus Theatre). He was a member of the Royal Court Young Writers' Group in 2013 and in 2014 he won the Channel 4 Playwrights' Scheme.

KATHERINE PEARCE | *Kate*

Katherine trained at the Royal Welsh College of Music and Drama..

Katherine's theatre credits include: *The Last Ballad of Lillian Billocca* (Hull Truck); *Low Level Panic* (Orange Tree Theatre); *Husbands and Sons, Port* (National Theatre); *Husbands and Sons, Our Pals* (Royal Exchange); *Secret Theatre Company: Stab in the Dark, Chamber Piece, Streetcar Named Desire, Woyzeck, A Series of Increasingly Impossible Acts, Glitterland* (Lyric Hammersmith).

Television credits include: *Girlfriends, Vera* (ITV); *Three Girls, Young Hyacinth, Our Girl* (BBC).

Film credits include: *My Cousin Rachel* (Fox Searchlight); *England Is Mine* (HonlodgeProductions); *The Last Photograph* (The Works International).

CHARLOTTE O'LEARY | *Sam/Alex/Liv*

Charlotte Trained at the Royal Welsh College of Music and Drama.

Theatre credits include: *Under Milk Wood* (Watermill Theatre); *Hush* (Paines Plough); *Three Days in the Country* (Richard Burton Theatre); *Dying for It, The Two Gentleman of Verona, Three Sisters* (Richard Burton Theatre Company).

Radio credits include: *Torchwood* (Big Finish Productions).

JACK WILKINSON | *Pete/Dave/Will*

Jack trained at Drama Centre London.

Theatre includes: *Twelfth Night* (Shakespeare's Globe); *King Lear* (Northern Broadsides/UK tour); *Close the Coalhouse Door* (Northern Stage/UK tour); *Dreamplay* (The Vaults/ HighTide); *David Copperfield* (Oldham Coliseum, nominated for Best Actor at MTA Awards); *All of Me* (The Vaults); *Grimms Ditch* (Print Works); *Larisa and the Merchants* (Arcola); *Deadkidsongs* (Theatre Royal Bath) and *The Good Soul of Szechuan* (Watford Palace Theatre).

Television credits include: *Holby City, Doctors* (BBC) and *Marvellous* (Tiger Aspect).

Film credits include: *The Love Punch* (Radar Films).

Radio credits include: *Close the Coalhouse Door* (BBC).

STEF O'DRISCOLL | *Direction*

Stef is the Artistic Director of nabokov and was previously Associate Director at Paines Plough and at the Lyric Hammersmith.

For Paines Plough: *With a Little Bit of Luck* by Sabrina Mahfouz; *Hopelessly Devoted* by Kate Tempest; *Blister* by Laura Lomas; and as Assistant Director: *Wasted* by Kate Tempest.

For nabokov: *Last Night* by Benin City (Roundhouse/Latitude); *Box Clever* by Monsay Whiney (Marlowe Theatre/Roundabout); *Storytelling Army* (Brighton Festival); and *Slug* by Sabrina Mahfouz (Latitude).

For the Lyric, as Co Director: *A Midsummer Night's Dream;* as Associate Director: *Mogadishu* (Manchester Royal Exchange); as Assistant Director: *Blasted* (winner Olivier Award for Outstanding Achievement in an Affiliate Theatre 2011).

Other Director credits: *Yard Gal* by Rebecca Prichard (Oval House, winner Fringe Report Award for Best Fringe Production 2009), *A Tale from The Bedsit* by Paul Cree (Roundhouse/Bestival); *Finding Home* by Cecilia Knapp (Roundhouse); *A Guide to Second Date Sex* and *When Women Wee* (Underbelly/Soho); and as Assistant Director: *Henry IV* (Donmar/St Anne's Warehouse).

JENNIFER JACKSON | *Co-Movement Director*

Jennifer trained at East 15 and is a movement director and actor.

Movement direction includes: *Queens of the Coal Age* (Royal Exchange); *Brighton Rock (*Pilot Theatre); *Parliament* Square (The Bush, Royal Exchange); *Our Town* (Royal Exchange); *The Mountaintop* (Young Vic); *Out Of Love/Black Mountain/How to Be a Kid* (Paines Plough, Orange Tree Theatre, Theatr Clwyd and Roundabout tour); *Kika's Birthday* (Orange Tree Theatre); *Death of a Salesman* (Royal & Derngate); *The Ugly One* (The Park 90); *Phone Home* (Shoreditch Town Hall); *Why the Whales Came* (Southbank Centre); *Stone Face* (Finborough Theatre); *Debris* (Southwark Playhouse/Openworks Theatre); *Macbeth* (Passion in Practice, Sam Wanamaker Playhouse); *Silent Planet* (Finborough); *Pericles* (Berwaldhallen); *The Future* (The Yard/Company Three); *Other-Please Specify, Atoms* (Company Three).

As a performer she has worked with National Theatre, Bath Theatre Royal, Royal & Derngate, Lyric Hammersmith, Shoreditch Town Hall, Derby Theatre, Birmingham Rep, Southwark Playhouse and the Sam Wanamaker Playhouse. She is currently touring Bryony Lavery's adaptation of *Brighton Rock*.

PETER SMALL | *Lighting*

Peter studied Lighting Design at RADA.

Recent productions as Lighting Designer include: *Plastic* (Poleroid Theatre, Old Red Lion); *All or Nothing* (West End and UK tour); *Old Fools* (Southwark Playhouse); *Out of Love, Black Mountain* (Offie Nominated) and *How to Be a Kid* (Paines Plough/Orange Tree); *A Girl in School Uniform (Walks Into A Bar)* (New Diorama, Offie nominated); *Fox* (Old Red Lion); *Memory of Leaves* (UK tour); *East End Boys and West End Girls* (Arcola Theatre and UK tour); *Electric and Politrix* (Big House Theatre); *Tom and Jerry* (EventBox Theatre, Egypt); *Cinderella* (Loughborough); and *The Venus Factor* (Bridewell Theatre).

DOMINIC KENNEDY | *Sound and Composition*

Dominic Kennedy is a Sound Designer and Music Producer for performance and live events. He has a keen interest in developing new work and implementing sound and music at an early stage in a creative process. Dominic is a graduate from Royal Central School of Speech and Drama where he developed specialist skills in collaborative and devised theatre making, music composition and installation practices. His work often fuses found sound, field recordings, music composition and synthesis.

Recent design credits include: *The Assasination of Katie Hopkins* (Theatre Clwyd); *Roundabout Season* 2017 (Paines Plough); *With a Little Bit of Luck* (Paines Plough); *Ramona Tells Jim* (Bush Theatre); *And the Rest of Me Floats* (Outbox); *I Am a Tree* (Jamie Wood); *Box Clever* (nabokov); *Skate Hard Turn Left* (Battersea Arts Centre); *Gap in the Light* (Engineer); *Broken Biscuits* (Paines Plough); Roundabout Season 2016 (Paines Plough); *The Devil Speaks True* (Goat and Monkey); *Run* (Engineer) and *Ono* (Jamie Wood).

SIMON CARROLL-JONES | *Co-Movement Director*

Simon trained at East 15 Acting School. He is a theatre maker, Movement Director and actor.

Movement Direction includes: *The Act* (The Yard/Company 3); *Bear and Butterfly* (Dani Parr and Theatre Hullabaloo); *Spring Awakening / Marigolds* (Brockley Jack/Outfox); *The Cycle Play* (East 15); *+ – Human Response* (Roundhouse); *Tricycle Takeover/Mapping Brent* (The Tricycle).

Simon has taught movement at Central School of Speech and Drama, East 15 Acting School, and Identity Acting School.

As an actor Simon has worked with the RSC, Soho Theatre, The Royal & Derngate, Bath Theatre Royal, Shoreditch Town Hall, Tangled Feet Theatre, Theatre Hullabaloo, Hull Truck, Lyric Hammersmith, Battersea Arts Centre, Oval House. He is an associate artist of Angel Exit Theatre, Moving Dust, Tangled Feet and Upstart Theatre.

Simon's solo show *Marco* will be touring in 2019 with James Blakey and Upstart Theatre.

BALISHA KARRA | *Assistant Director*

Balisha studies at University of Birmingham (BA Hons in Drama and Theatre Arts).

Trainee Assistant Director: *A Midsummer Night's Dream* (Young Vic, supported by Boris Karloff Foundation).

Assistant Director: *Present Laughter* (Chichester Theatre Fesitval), *Freeman* by Strictly Arts (Belgrade Theatre Company UK tour, supported by Regional Theatre Young Directors Scheme).

Director Credits: *Besharam* Project R&D (Derby Theatre); *Tamasha Scratch Night* (Writers Group/RichMix)l and Foundry Director for shows including *Mr Muscle*, *West* and *Confetti* (Birmingham REP).

CAITLIN O'REILLY | *Company Stage Manager*

Caitlin is a freelance events/productions professional and has been working as a stage manager for the past nine years.

Credits include: *Suppliant Women* (Actors Touring Company, Hong Kong Arts Festival); *Romeo and Juliet* (Orange Tree Theatre); *Beauty and the Beast* (Chichester Festival Theatre); *Dry Room* (Eldarin Young, Taiwan World Stage Design Festival); *Running Wild* (Michael Morpurgo, national tour); *Goosebumps Alive* (Tom Salamon, Vaults, Waterloo); *I Know All the Secrets in My World* (Tiata Fahodzi, national tour); *The 39 Steps* (Patrick Barlow, Criterion Theatre) and *Ben Hur* (Patrick Barlow, Tricycle Theatre), among many more.

PAINES PLOUGH

Paines Plough is the UK's national theatre of new plays. We commission and produce the best playwrights and tour their plays far and wide. Whether you're in Swansea or Sheffield, Glasgow or Gloucester, a Paines Plough show is coming to a theatre near you soon.

'The lifeblood of the UK's theatre ecosystem' Guardian

Paines Plough was formed in 1974 over a pint of Paines Bitter in The Plough pub. Since then we've produced more than 130 new productions by world renowned playwrights like Stephen Jeffreys, Abi Morgan, Sarah Kane, Mark Ravenhill, Dennis Kelly, Mike Bartlett and Kate Tempest. We've toured those plays to hundreds of places from Brisbane to Bristol to Belfast.

'That noble company Paines Plough, de facto
national theatre of new writing' Daily Telegraph

In the past three years we've produced 30 shows and performed them in over 200 places across four continents. We tour to more than 30,000 people a year from Cornwall to the Orkney Islands, in village halls and Off-Broadway, at music festivals and student unions, online and on radio, and in our own pop-up theatre Roundabout.

With Programme 2018 we continue to tour the length and breadth of the UK from clubs and pubs to lakeside escapes and housing estates. Roundabout hosts a jam-packed Edinburgh Festival Fringe programme and brings mini-festivals to each stop on its nationwide tour, and you can even catch us on screen with *Every Brilliant Thing* available on Sky Atlantic and HBO.

Our 'Come to Where I'm From' smartphone app is available free on iOS and Android, featuring 160 short audio plays from Olivier Award winners to first-time writers.

'I think some theatre just saved my life.'
@kate_clement on Twitter

PAINES PLOUGH **ROUNDABOUT**

'A beautifully designed masterpiece in engineering . . . a significant breakthrough in theatre technology' The Stage

Roundabout is Paines Plough's beautiful portable in-the-round theatre. It's a completely self-contained 168-seat auditorium that flat-packs into a single lorry and pops up anywhere from theatres to school halls, sports centres, warehouses, car parks and fields.

We built Roundabout to enable us to tour to places that don't have theatres. For the next decade Roundabout will travel the length and breadth of the UK bringing the nation's best playwrights and a thrilling theatrical experience to audiences everywhere.

Over the last five years, Roundabout has toured the four corners of the UK hosting over 2,000 hours of entertainment for more than 100,000 people.

Roundabout was designed by Lucy Osborne and Emma Chapman at Studio Three Sixty in collaboration with Charcoalblue and Howard Eaton.

Winner of Theatre Building of the Year
at The Stage Awards 2014

'Roundabout venue wins most beautiful
interior venue by far @edfringe'
@ChaoticKirsty on Twitter

'Roundabout is a beautiful, magical space. Hidden tech make it
Turkish-bath-tranquil but with circus-tent cheek. Aces.'
@evenicol on Twitter

Roundabout was made possible thanks to the belief and generous support of the following trusts and individuals and all who named a seat in Roundabout. We thank them all.

TRUSTS AND FOUNDATIONS

Andrew Lloyd Webber Foundation

Paul Hamlyn Foundation

Garfield Weston Foundation

J Paul Getty Jnr Charitable Trust

John Ellerman Foundation

Universal Consolidated Group

CORPORATE

Howard Eaton Lighting Ltd

Charcoalblue

Avolites Ltd

John Ellerman Foundation

Factory Settings

Total Solutions

Pop your name on a seat and help us pop-up around the UK:

www.justgiving.com/fundraising/roundaboutauditorium

Paines Plough

Theatr Clwyd

*'One of the hidden treasures of North Wales,
a huge vibrant culture complex'* Guardian

Theatr Clwyd is one of the foremost producing theatres in Wales – a beacon of excellence looking across the Clwydian Hills yet only forty minutes from Liverpool.

Since 1976 it has been a theatrical powerhouse and much-loved home for the community. Now, led by the Executive team of Tamara Harvey and Liam Evans-Ford, it is going from strength to strength producing world-class theatre, from new plays to classic revivals.

There are three theatre spaces, a cinema, café, bar and art galleries and, alongside its own shows, it offers a rich and varied programme of visual arts, film, theatre, music, dance and comedy. Theatr Clwyd works extensively with the local community, schools and colleges and creates award-winning work for, with and by young people. In the past two years it has co-produced with the Sherman Theatre, Hijinx, Gagglebabble and The Other Room in Cardiff, Paines Plough, Vicky Graham Productions, HighTide, Hampstead Theatre, Bristol Old Vic, the Rose Theatre, Kingston, Headlong, Sheffield Theatres, the Orange Tree Theatre, English Touring Theatre and National Theatre, among others.

In 2016/17 over 420,000 people saw a Theatr Clwyd production, in the building and across the UK.

Island Town

Characters

Kate
Sam
Pete
Dave
Alex
Will
Liv

The play is set in a town in the middle of the countryside. A town large enough to have a ring road going around it, but not that much in the middle.

Kate is played by one person. Sam, Alex and Liv are played by another. Pete, Dave and Will by another.

One

Kate Because I don't think you'll care about me at the end. If I tell you what I've done. I don't think you'll care about me. Or like me. But standing here. Standing in front of you. In this dead town that I grew up in. I can't think about anything else. It all just circles round the inside of my head. And won't let me go. So maybe if I tell you it will. Maybe if I say it all out loud again it'll let me go. So I think I'll do that.

You probably won't like me. But maybe you will. I won't mind either way. I just want it to let me go.

Because then.

Because then maybe I'll – I'll be able to start again.

Two

Pete Where from?

Kate What you just said?

Sam About what he did?

Kate Yeah.

Pete Don't tell her though.

Sam Why?

Pete Dunno because –

Sam Because what?

Pete It's a bit weird thinking about it now.

Sam Thinking about it now?

Pete Yeah?

Sam But not at the time?

Pete Yeah I guess both.

Sam   I'm telling her.

Kate   Tell me what?

Pete   Ah yeah go on it's kind of funny actually.

Kate   What is?

Sam   Last week right?

Kate   Yeah?

Sam   Know what he did?

Kate   No what?

Sam   Tell her.

Pete   You tell her.

Sam   He pulled my grandma.

Kate   What?

Sam   Like just properly grabbed her face and just started kissing her.

Kate   What?

Sam   Tongue and all.

Kate   That true?

Pete   It is yeah.

Sam   It was one of the funniest things I've ever seen.

Kate   Talking shite.

Sam   I'm not.

Pete   She's not.

Kate   Why?

Pete   Why what?

Kate   Why'd you get off with her nan what else mate?

Pete   Dunno. Just wanted to see what it was like.

Kate   Can you not imagine?

Pete   Nah not really.

Kate   Not really?

Pete   No. How would I do that?

Kate   Just imagine getting off with someone but make that person old that's how you do it mate.

Pete   Yeah but.

Kate   But what?

Pete   Not the same is it?

Kate   Bollocks you did. He being funny?

Sam   Ask him.

Kate   You being funny?

Pete   No.

Kate   And you see this happen?

Sam   Yeah.

Kate   Not want to stop it?

Sam   Told you.

Kate   What?

Sam   Was funny. Why would I stop that?

Kate   Messed up in the head you.

Sam   Why's that then?

Pete   Not you. Him. Actually you and all letting him do it.

Sam   Was so funny. He was like shall I do it? And I was like yeah why not.

Kate   That it?

Sam   What?

Kate   Not a bet or something?

Pete   No why's there need to be a bet?

Kate   So you would come out of this a tiny bit better than you are at the moment because right now all it is is that you've pulled her nan just because you fancied doing it.

Pete   I was very drunk.

Sam   He was.

Kate   Why were you both drunk around your nan?

Sam   Family barbeque.

Kate   He's not your family.

Sam   Nah but asked him to come.

Kate   Why?

Sam   Dunno.

Kate   What about me?

Sam   Thought you'd be busy.

Kate   Why'd you think that?

Sam   Dunno because –

Kate   How'd you know he wasn't busy?

Sam   He's never busy is he? And it's different isn't it because of your –

Kate   How'd it happen then?

Sam   Said. Just thought it would be funny.

Kate   Funny?

Sam   Yeah.

Kate   That it?

Pete   What more you want?

Sam   He just goes shall I get with your nan? I went yeah go on. And he goes she's quite fit isn't she like for a nan and then –

Pete   I just go over to her and am like alright how're you not said hello to you yet and she just kind of looks at me and then I just give her a big old kiss on the lips and then go in with my tongue which is a bit weird but I went with it and then stopped and was like alright? And after that she's looking at me still and then just goes and who are you then and I'm like I'm Pete nice to meet you and she was like you're very friendly and I went thanks very much and then that was that. Was quality. First kiss that.

Kate   Yeah sounds quality.

Pete   Next time I'll be ready for someone my own age whose teeth feel a bit like firmer in place.

Kate   Jesus. She knows you're only fifteen right?

Pete   Dunno why?

Kate   Dunno doesn't that make her like – I dunno. A paedo?

Sam   Don't think my nan's one of them.

Kate   Might be never know.

Sam   Think we would.

Kate   Yeah I guess and he did come on to her.

Sam   And she didn't know what was happening.

Kate   That can be her defence then.

Sam   My dad chucked him out a bit after that.

Kate   Did he see you kissing her?

Sam   No.

Kate   Why'd he throw you out then?

Sam   Because he got naked and just started paddling about in the fish pond.

Kate   What?

Pete   Seemed like a good idea at the time.

Sam   Was funny too.

Kate   Why'd you –

Pete   Was a bit hot.

Kate   So?

Pete   Thought it would cool me down. Summer and that isn't it? Boiling. And drank a load of her dad's whisky and all.

Sam   He was standing in the pond just going I'm hot it's hot I just want to be cooler I think I'm dying I think I'm going to die.

Pete   Bit dramatic but worked and all because I didn't die and did cool me down and all. But then her dad got proper mad and I think goes like get that spitpiss out of my pond right now and then I go they're moving under me the fish are moving and then I go I've broken one Sam I've broken one of the fish and I pick up this dead fish right and go Sam look it's a tragedy I've caused the tragedy here and her dad he flips right and just legs it over to me right and I'm still standing naked in this pond holding a dead fish and he just picks me up and carries me to the gate and lobs me in the street and then I'm just on the pavement which is boiling and all burning my arse and that and then I just went home.

Kate   Fucksake that's not true.

Sam   All true. Funny that.

Kate   Bollocks is it.

Sam   Not making it up.

Pete   Still got this fish and all. Took him home and put him in a saucepan. Thought I could resurrect it but I couldn't resurrect it.

Kate   Invite me next time?

Sam   Yeah alright. Told you thought you'd be busy.

Kate   Why?

Sam   With your dad?

Kate   Any more drink?

Pete   Not much. Actually not –

Sam   Where'd you get it?

Kate   Home.

Sam   He won't notice?

Kate   Have a guess?

Pete   Can he not drink or something?

Kate   Can't do anything.

Pete   What anything?

Kate   No.

Sam   Not that bad is he?

Kate   Can talk and move around a bit. Sometimes eats and sometimes has a drink then goes to the toilet.

Pete   That's fucking loads then.

Sam   Is it shite?

Pete   Made it out like he was a potato or something.

Kate   Know what I meant.

Sam   Is he alright?

Pete   Wish my brother was a potato and all. And his girlfriend.

Sam   She moved in yet?

Pete   Yeah. It's terrible. She smells like an egg.

Sam   Is he alright though?

Kate   What?

Sam   Asked if he was alright.

Kate   Who?

Sam   Your dad? Who else?

Kate   He's fine.

Sam   Is he?

Kate   Has to be doesn't he? Pass that cider.

Pete   Tried to tell you. None left.

. . .

Sam   I can get some this week.

Kate   Where from?

Sam   Give us some money and I'll get it from the shop.

Kate   What? Just nick it?

Sam   Alright for not losing my job thanks.

Kate   Shit job anyway.

Sam   Better than nothing isn't it?

Kate   Not even a proper job anyway is it?

Sam   I work. For money. That's a job.

Kate   Fifiteen though. Kiddie wage that.

Sam   Sixteen next year.

Kate   Oh right then what? Full time at the newsagent is it?
Sounds a laugh.

Sam   Better than nothing. Pays for you to get pissed
doesn't it?

Kate   Need something now.

Sam   Can't help you with that.

Kate   I'll get Pete to nick some from his brother.

Sam   Yeah do that then.

Kate   Reckon he'll be mad with me?

Sam   Who?

Kate   His brother?

Sam   Why? What you do?

Kate   Dunno always do something to wind him up don't I? How're your mum and dad?

Sam   Shit.

Kate   Kicking off at each other again or something?

Sam   Yeah a bit.

Kate   That's funny.

Sam   Is it?

Kate   Dunno. Kind of.

Sam   Keep waking my little sister up.

Kate   Why?

Sam   Shouting at each other all night.

Kate   They smack each other?

Sam   A bit.

Kate   That's funny.

Sam   Is it?

Kate   Dunno. Parents scrapping with each other. Think that's funny.

. . .

Pete   Couldn't get any.

Kate   Why not?

Pete   Brother was stomping about the house like a bellend.

Sam   Why?

Pete   Got his girlfriend pregnant.

Sam   What?

Pete   He's having a baby.

Sam   Not happy about it?

Pete   No. No one would be. Jesus. Seen the state of his girlfriend? Imagine being stuck with that. And then a smaller version of it.

Kate   Got nothing then?

Pete   What?

Kate   Said you would bring drink?

Pete   That all you care about? Just said I'm going to be an uncle and you're only interested in getting pissed.

Kate   Right yeah congratulations and that but seriously where's the –

Pete   Told you.

Kate   Told me what?

Pete   That I couldn't get –

Kate   Told you he'd fuck it up didn't I?

Pete   Alright mate calm down I got some just joking wasn't I? So angry you.

Kate   Yeah?

Pete   Yeah said I would didn't I?

Kate   Where's it from?

Pete   Brother's room. Keeps it under his bed. Legged it in when he was taking an angry piss. Mad that. Was just in the bog taking a slash and screaming like he was pissing out lava from his knob or something.

Sam   Is she keeping it?

Pete   Yeah.

Sam   Baby's going to help with his rage isn't it?

Pete   Won't be any different will it? Angriest man in the world isn't he? Imagine if you two got together hey?

Kate   Why?

Pete   Because if that happened and you had a kid it would be like a more violent Satan.

Kate   I'm alright for sleeping with your brother thanks.

Pete   Yeah probably a good idea given the current state of things and anyway and he's still pissed off with you and all.

Sam   Why?

Kate   Why?

Pete   Why?

Kate   Yeah why?

Pete   Why'd you think?

Kate   Dunno.

Pete   Threw up on his car didn't you?

Kate   Oh that. Fucksake. Was ages ago. And was only the wheel wasn't it?

Pete   He loves the wheels in particular.

Sam   What?

Pete   Just got them done. Was telling me about them. You ever listened to someone talk about car wheels before? Fuck me that's boring. I mean. They look the same as before but apparently they're different. He loves them though.

Kate   He'll get over it.

Pete   He won't though will he? We all know my brother. He doesn't get over anything. Does he? He's full of rage. Angriest man in the world. Should have seen him when I nearly burned the house down.

Sam   What?

Pete   What?

Kate   What you say?

Pete   About what?

Kate   You nearly burned your house down?

Pete   Yeah.

Sam   What?

Pete   What?

Kate   What's that about then?

Pete   What's what about?

Kate   Burning your house down?

Pete   What about it?

Kate   Yeah.

Pete   Did I not tell you this?

Sam   No.

Pete   Oh right sorry forgot. Yeah I nearly burned my house down.

Kate   Why?

Pete   Cremating that fish I killed in her pond.

Sam   Cremating a fish?

Pete   Yeah.

Kate   From her pond?

Pete   Yeah.

Sam   Still had that?

Pete   Yeah. Was in the freezer.

Sam   Why?

Pete   Because I put it there.

Sam   Why?

Pete   Dunno can't remember now. But anyway I felt guilty so decided to cremate it you know? Just to send it off to fish

heaven or whatever. So did that but did it with petrol which
I think was a bit violent for one goldfish because I didn't
know how much to use so used probably too much and the
fish exploded.

Kate   What like blew up?

Pete   Yeah blew up. It blew up. The fish exploded. Then
my brother looked out the window and was like what the fuck
are you playing at? And I said I just cremated a fish but then
we had to call the fire brigade because the garden table was
on fire quite a lot.

Sam   Quite a lot?

Pete   Well it was on fire enough for the house to catch fire
a bit too.

Sam   A bit?

Pete   Just a bit. But if your house is on fire just a bit then
that I guess that means it's just on fire so probably not what
anyone's after although I thought a fire engine was a bit over
the top but guess you got to be careful with fire don't you?

Kate   You set your house on fire because you were trying to
cremate a goldfish?

Pete   Yeah. Bit mad right? Anyway they came and squirted
the fire out and I asked to have a go on the hose and they said
no because they were busy trying to stop my house being on
fire which they did and then everything was alright after that
and the fish was no longer to be seen along with the table
which my brother wasn't massively happy about but it was all
worth it because the fish is now smoke drifting on the breeze
like the sky was its new ocean or something. Brother was
raging. Smacked me a bit after that. Why my face is all
bruised up. Cut my lip too. Broke a tooth. Guess I deserved
that right? But yeah. Hope having a baby calms him down.
I don't think it will though. Can I tell you something? I'm
well jealous of him having a baby. Would love that me.

. . .

Kate   What you doing?

Sam   Nothing. Felt like a walkabout.

Kate   Any more of them?

Sam   Help yourself.

Kate   Whose are these?

Sam   Mum's.

Kate   Nick them?

Sam   Not really. Just lying around. She was out. Taste like shit.

Kate   Better than nothing hey? Got a lighter?

Sam   Yeah.

Kate   What's up with you?

Sam   Nothing much. Just had to get out the house.

Kate   Why?

Sam   Parents going at it. Thought Dad was going to rip my mum's head off.

Kate   In a funny way like?

Sam   Have a guess.

Kate   What's that in there?

Sam   In what?

Kate   That bag?

Sam   My little sister.

Kate   What?

Sam   Have a look. She's asleep.

Kate   Put your little sister in a bag?

Sam   Would have had to go through Mum and Dad to get the pushchair. She's alright.

Kate Walking about with a kiddie in a bag in the middle
of the night?

Sam Didn't want her to hear it all.

Kate She won't remember.

Sam No. But I will though.

Kate Still though. Get nicked for that?

Sam Putting a kid in a bag? Don't think so. And anyway
not like she's dead and in a supermarket carrier bag. She's
fine. Made it comfy for her.

Kate Yeah?

Sam Wouldn't mind someone carrying me about like that.

Kate Yeah?

Sam Be like being in a nice soft cave.

Kate Yeah I guess. We're too big for that though.

. . .

Kate How'd you do?

Pete Have a guess?

Kate Shite?

Pete Shite. Spot on. She did alright.

Kate Yeah?

Sam I guess. Not really. You?

Kate Dunno don't care really.

Pete What we do now?

Sam What you mean?

Pete When you finish school? What do you do when
you've got no one telling you what to do?

Kate Dunno. Do whatever you want.

Pete   Yeah?

Kate   Yeah.

Pete   Alright. What should I do now? Let's have a think. Alright reckon I should try and have sex with someone.

Kate   Yeah?

Pete   Yeah. Sixteen and that. I'm now legal. Watch out Pete's about. That's good isn't it? Not done it before. So. So that's something to try and do isn't it? That's normal isn't it?

Kate   Need someone to have sex with for that which is a problem for you.

Pete   Yeah yeah yeah yeah. Need to sort that out. How'd I do it?

Sam   Not going to explain to you how to –

Pete   Not that. Meant find someone.

Kate   Find a hospital for the blind and hang about there.

Pete   Must be someone about.

Kate   Not in this town.

Pete   There's one in the supermarket.

Sam   One?

Pete   She's alright. Keep trying to talk to her. Maybe she'll do.

Sam   Lucky girl.

Pete   Yeah trying with her. Keep buying stuff but she doesn't seem that bothered.

Sam   Are you speaking to her?

Pete   When?

Sam   When you're buying things?

Pete   No. Why?

Sam   Because you might want to talk to her.

Pete   Why?

Kate   Because that's how this works mate isn't it? Because if you're just buying stuff and not talking to her you're not flirting or cracking on with her you're just. Shopping.

Pete   Nah I'm being subtle.

Sam   How?

Pete   With the things I buy.

Sam   What do you buy?

Pete   Dunno. Things and that. Pack of six sausages.

Kate   What? Why?

Pete   Didn't know what else to buy. And thought. You know.

Kate   You know what?

Pete   They're quite like. Dunno.

Kate   Quite what?

Pete   Suggestive.

Sam   Suggestive?

Pete   Yeah.

Kate   Of what?

Pete   You know.

Kate   He's – Am I thinking this right?

Sam   Think so.

Kate   Did you think buying a six pack of sausages would be suggestive because a sausage looks like a dick?

Pete   Yeah. But it didn't work I don't think.

Kate   Yeah no shit. Walking up to someone suggestively placing what essentially looks like six severed penises wrapped in plastic in front of them to try and chat them up didn't work?

Pete   Alright alright I don't know. I don't know what I'm doing do I? This is shit. Everything's too hard isn't it? Why's everything so hard? Stuck in this town not knowing what to do. Everything's much harder than it should be isn't it?

Sam   If you do stuff like that then yeah.

Pete   Tell me then.

Sam   What?

Pete   What to do?

Sam   I don't know.

Pete   Maybe we should do that thing?

Sam   What thing?

Pete   Where we like make a pact that by the time we're like a certain age then we could –

Kate   No. Shut up.

Pete   What?

Kate   Talking like that. No one does shite like that. You think they do because you're a idiot. But no one does.

Pete   But what if we're all on our own –

Kate   No mate. Stop talking. That will never happen. Sleeping with you? I don't think I can think of anything worse. No disrespect and that and you're my best mate and that and I love you and stuff but having sex with you. I mean. I think that would. Like. Dunno. I think if I did that then it would make me. Like. Violent. Like it would happen and the next day I think I would just be like I've got to kill something. I need to kill. Something. Anything. I have to kill something. Then just start small like ants and flies and that. Just kill them a lot. But realise that's not satisfying this violent urge so then just move up to mice and that. Then cats and dogs. Then. Dunno. A pig? Then a cow and then a horse or something. But it wouldn't be enough. So then I'll just go on to humans. Just violently kill humans. And kids. And babies. In one day.

All that killing in one day which happens to be the one after we had sex.

Pete   Right well that's the confidence boost that I –

Sam   I wouldn't either.

Pete   Right yeah thanks.

Sam   I would feel the same –

Pete   Yeah alright –

Sam   I would feel like committing horrible acts of violence because I saw your pe –

Pete   Alright shut up about it it was just an idea. Not that bad am I?

Kate   Look a bit like a fish so –

Pete   Alright shut up. But not being funny or anything but that's all you need isn't it?

Kate   What?

Pete   A family.

Kate   A family?

Pete   Reckon I should give that a go. All you need isn't it?

Kate   A decent one.

Pete   Yeah mine will be. Be the best family you've ever seen. Just laugh all the time. Thirty kids legging it about. Be amazing. Wouldn't ever be bored then would you? Just be constantly legging it about after them all. Be like what's that one doing climbing in the oven? And why's the other one switching the grill on? Better turn that off but can't because one's killing the dog with a kitchen knife. Oh what's going on over there why's that one wearing. Like. A hat? Or something. Where'd that come from? Never seen that hat before. I mean. You'd never be bored. That is my dream.

Kate   Sounds terrible.

Pete   Yeah no shit that sounds terrible to you.

Kate   Why's that then?

Pete   You'd be terrible.

Kate   At what?

Pete   Being a mum.

Kate   What you saying?

Pete   Saying if you ever have a kid then poor kid.

Kate   Fuck off.

Sam   He's got a point.

Kate   Has he?

Sam   Still don't know my little sister's name do you?

Kate   Yeah I do.

Sam   What is it then?

Kate   Sandra.

Sam   Sandra?

Kate   Yeah.

Sam   Sandra?

Kate   Yeah that's her name isn't it?

Sam   No. That's not even close. Where'd you get Sandra from? My little sister is not called Sandra. No one is called Sandra.

Pete   Except. Like. Cleaners and that.

Sam   She's called Alex.

Kate   Yeah knew that didn't I?

Pete   Why'd you say Sandra then?

Kate   Just joking wasn't I?

Pete   You weren't though were –

Kate   Alright got mixed up shut up about it.

Pete   See.

Kate   What?

Pete   Be terrible. You'll keep forgetting their names and then eventually forget them literally.

Kate   I'd be alright.

Pete   Bollocks you would. Be drunk all the time. You'd be a classic drunk mum.

Sam   You'd kill your kid in a car crash.

Kate   Jesus that's nice.

Pete   She's got a point and all.

Kate   You'd be a shite dad.

Pete   You know and I know and Sam knows that's not true. I'd be amazing. The best. Just need someone to do it with.

Sam   You could go out with my nan? She might be a bit old for physically producing kids though. But. You know. Worth a try?

Pete   I don't think I want to go out with your nan thanks.

Sam   She'll be devastated but will recover.

Pete   Mean it though.

Kate   Mean what?

Pete   That's all I want. Think about it all the time. Get jealous of my big brother about it.

Kate   Why?

Pete   Why what?

Kate   What's your brother got to do with it?

Pete   Oh my God are you being funny mate? How pissed are you? Told you so many times. Keep talking about it don't I? He's going to have a baby isn't he? Told you about three hundred times haven't I? Keep talking about it? His girlfriend is pregnant and will produce a tiny ugly baby and because of that I will become an uncle because you know that's how life works isn't it? Are you losing it? Can't remember things? First case in history of a teenager getting fucking dementia.

Kate   Alright calm down just –

Pete   Not fair. None of it is.

Sam   What isn't?

Pete   Him and his kid and all that. He's got all that and I've got nothing.

Sam   Takes time.

Pete   Does it?

Sam   I guess.

Pete   Horrible someone's done that isn't it?

Sam   What?

Pete   Shagged my brother. Makes me feel sick that.

Sam   You don't have to.

Pete   Know that don't I? Just the thought someone did. Even someone who smells that bad of egg should have standards above the state of my brother. Mental that. Anyway I'm sort of made up being an uncle though. Got a plan.

Kate   What's that?

Pete   Just going to give this kid so much love right then one day it'll just look at me and go Uncle Pete I wish you were my real dad.

Kate   Then what?

Pete   Then what what?

Sam   What happens when the kid's said that?

Pete   Dunno. Nick it and leg it off somewhere. Just make sure it's full of hope and that.

Kate   Jesus.

Pete   What?

Kate   Talking like that.

Pete   What's wrong with that?

Kate   Sound like a twat.

Pete   Alright –

Kate   Full of hope. Talking shit.

Pete   What you saying then?

Kate   Nothing much.

Pete   Exactly.

Kate   Don't get hope with families. And you don't get hope in towns like this. Get hope by yourself.

Pete   Sure.

Kate   That's what I'm doing.

Sam   What?

Kate   Out of here. This town. It's a prison. Not staying here and having a family. I'm leaving. Going. Get a car and drive for miles and miles and miles. Just keep going.

Pete   Get a car? That's funny.

Kate   How's that?

Pete   Sixteen aren't you? Have to be seventeen to drive. What you going to do? Just get a car now and just look at it for a year. Besides be boring having a car.

Kate   Why's that then?

Pete   Can't drink then can you?

Kate   Yeah you can. Five and drive.

Pete   Five and drive? Fuck's that?

Kate   Five pints and you're alright. Everyone out here gets pissed and drives. Otherwise what the fuck else is there to do?

Sam   What happens when you get to the sea?

Kate   What?

Sam   On a tiny island aren't we? Keep driving you'll end up at the sea. Then what?

Kate   Keep going somehow. I'll figure it out when I get there.

Pete   Right yeah your car turn into a boat and all?

Kate   Said.

Sam   Said what?

Kate   Figure something out.

Sam   And who's going to look after your dad?

Kate   Got a carer doesn't he?

Sam   What happens when that goes?

Kate   How's that going to go? Don't think anyone's going to be like oh we should get rid of people making home visits to people that are dying in their own houses to save a bit of cash. Won't happen will it?

Pete   Home though isn't it?

Kate   What?

Pete   This town. Got each other don't we? And that's what home is. I think anyway. Not buildings or parks or roads or anything. Just people isn't it?

Kate   Well there you go then.

Pete   What?

Kate   Home can be anywhere then can't it? So why the fuck are we here? Need more to drink.

Pete   Got no money.

Kate   Nick it off your brother again?

Pete   He'd kill me.

Kate   You?

Sam   Don't get paid till next week.

Kate   Oh well I'll just nick some off my dad.

Sam   Won't notice?

Kate   Probably not. And who gives a shit if he does?

. . .

Pete   Get it?

Kate   Yeah.

Sam   How much?

Kate   Thirty or something.

Pete   No change?

Kate   Change? Don't get change from a drug dealer do you? Seen one carrying a till about have you? Asking if you need the receipt and that.

Pete   What is it?

Kate   Bit of weed is all. What's that?

Pete   What's it look like?

Kate   A pumpkin.

Pete   Yeah it is a pumpkin. Well identified mate.

Kate   What for?

Pete   What for what?

Kate   What for what for what? Why you got a fucking pumpkin?

Pete   You thick? Carve a face in it. Be well spooky that.

Kate   How old are you?

Pete   Sixteen why?

Kate   Kiddies do that.

Pete   Oh you're too old for this then?

Kate   Dunno bit stupid.

Pete   You're fucking stupid and all. Give us that cider.

Sam   Where you going to put it?

Pete   Gonna carve a spooky little face in it right and then hang it outside the door of the house so when my brother opens the door it'll be right in his face and he'll be like oh fucking hell what's that and scare him so much so he falls over and smacks his head open on the front step so his brain leaks out his skull and then he's dead.

Kate   Good plan that.

Pete   Yeah thought so. Then he'd be gone and I wouldn't get done for murder and all that shite.

Sam   The perfect crime.

Pete   Exactly. Want to help me do it?

Kate   No.

Pete   There's a surprise. You?

Sam   What?

Pete   Pumpkin?

Sam   What about it?

Pete   Help me do a face in it.

Sam   When?

Pete   Now.

Sam   Need a knife.

Pete   Yeah got one here. Want to help?

Kate   What you carrying a knife about for?

Pete   Carving pumpkins and that. Give us a hand be a laugh.

Sam   You're alright I'll watch.

Pete   Suit yourself. Sure you don't want a go?

Kate   No. Pass that cider.

Pete   How'd you do it?

Sam   Do what?

Pete   Make a face in it and that.

Sam   Cut off the top and then scoop out the middle and then make the face put a candle in light that then put the top back on.

Pete   Ah fuck it seems like too much effort actually. And you need a candle? No one's telling me that before. What's that for then to make the face light up or something?

Sam   Well worked out.

Pete   All that effort on a pumpkin? Mad that. Why's everything hard?

Sam   Not that hard –

Pete   Can you eat them instead?

Sam   If you like. Got to chop it up still.

Pete   What like the same as making it into a face?

Sam   Yeah.

Pete   Can't just eat it like it is no?

Sam   What like an apple or something?

Pete   Yeah.

Sam   No.

Pete   Ah fuck that an' all. Wasn't worth nicking was it?

Kate   You nick that?

Pete Yeah.

Kate Where from?

Pete Shop.

Kate Which one?

Pete Little one.

Sam One I work in?

Pete Yeah.

Sam What's wrong with you?

Pete What?

Sam Work there don't I?

Pete So?

Sam So what?

Pete That mean I can't nick stuff from there because you work there? Doesn't make sense does it?

Kate Should grass him in. Be funny.

Pete Don't do that.

Kate Then he'll get nicked.

Pete Nicked?

Kate Yeah. Get done for that. Shoplifting and that.

Pete Bollocks will you get done for nicking a pumpkin. What they going to do send me to prison?

Kate Might do.

Pete Oh yeah sure. Can imagine. Be locked up sitting about and one bloke's like I'm in here because I murdered all my kids with a brick what you done? I nicked a pumpkin mate let's share some feelings.

Kate Be funny if they did. Then all your life you can't get a job because you've got a criminal record for nicking a pumpkin. And eventually you run out of money and can't afford anything then you just kill yourself.

Pete   Yeah good story that mate liked the happy ending.

Kate   Could have nicked something more useful?

Pete   What drink?

Kate   Obviously.

Pete   Nah that was all behind the counter this was just out front so thought this was the easiest for a rob. Give us some of that.

Kate   Not much left.

Pete   Fuck off is there had like two sips.

Sam   Me too and all.

Pete   Not know how to share mate?

Kate   Keeping me warm.

Pete   Oh is that it is it? Should go to a pub then shouldn't we. Freezing tonight.

Kate   Pub's shite.

Pete   It's alright.

Kate   Which one?

Pete   Oak.

Kate   Oak's shite. Full of twats.

Pete   Better than the park isn't it? Three sixteen-year-olds in a kiddie park sharing a bottle of cider. We're doing alright aren't we?

Kate   I'm not complaining.

Pete   Yeah you not wonder why that is? Oh yeah because you've had about three litres of cider on your own.

Kate   Not pissed.

Pete   Bollocks are you not. I'm battered and I've had about two sips.

Sam   Do well in the pub then wouldn't you.

Pete   Yeah I'd get my head kicked in.

Sam   You going to be sick?

Kate   What?

Sam   Look like you are?

Kate   Do I shite. Worry about yourself.

Pete   What we doing next?

Sam   Dunno.

Pete   Can anyone give me a push on the swing?

Kate   Something wrong with you.

Pete   Oh too old for that an' all? Nothing else to do round here is there? Left school months ago. Done nothing except get pissed.

Kate   Nothing else to do.

Pete   Suppose. Oh forgot to tell you.

Sam   What?

Pete   My brother had his baby. I'm an uncle now.

. . .

Sam   Stop shouting alright.

Kate   Why? No one cares.

Sam   I do.

Kate   Why?

Sam   Because you'll wake her up?

Kate   Who?

Sam   My sister.

Kate So?

Sam What's it about anyway?

Kate What's what about?

Sam What you shouting at me for? And most people knock at the door normally anyway.

Kate Bored.

Sam So?

Kate So come out.

Sam Can't.

Kate Why not?

Sam Watching after my sister aren't I?

Kate Where's your dad?

Sam Out or something dunno.

Kate Be in the Oak getting pissed probably.

Sam Yeah probably.

Kate Pete said his brother said he's in there every night now.

Sam Not every night is it?

Kate Seems like he's coping really well with your mum walking out on you all.

Sam Yeah and how's your dad then? Dead yet?

Kate Come out with us we'll get pissed.

Sam Said I can't got to watch her don't I?

Kate She'll be fine. Said she was asleep and all.

Sam Right and what happens if she wakes up?

Kate Can look after herself can't she?

Sam She's five.

Kate   That's plenty old. Put her in the bag again.

Sam   Too heavy for that now.

Kate   What no she's not? Tiny.

Sam   Seen her recently?

Kate   Can walk can't she?

Sam   So?

Kate   So when kiddies can walk they can look after themselves right? If she gets into bother she can walk to the pub and tell your dad. Come out.

Sam   She could walk last year.

Kate   Oh right? Why were you carrying her about in a bag then?

Sam   Because it was the middle of the night and she was aslee – Why am I explaining this? I can't come out alright?

Kate   Nicked some vodka.

Sam   So?

Kate   So come drink it with me.

Sam   Go find Pete.

Kate   He's not about or he's not answering his door because he's wanking.

Sam   Oh yeah probably. You know he puts candles on while he does that?

Kate   What?

Sam   Says it makes it more romantic and less depressing.

Kate   Come out.

Sam   I told you –

Kate   Alright fuck's sake this shouldn't be happening you know?

Sam   What?

Kate   Your parents should be doing what you're doing now and we should be doing what they're probably doing now. Which is getting pissed.

Sam   Go do that then.

Kate   Do what?

Sam   Go get pissed. All you do anyway.

Kate   On my own?

Sam   Yeah.

Kate   I'm bored.

Sam   Well. Go home then.

Kate   Don't want to do that either.

Sam   Then dunno. Go do what Pete's doing.

Kate   What have a wank by candlelight?

Sam   Yeah that I don't care just leave me alone got to watch her. I'll be out tomorrow or something.

Kate   You telling me to just go have a –

Sam   Yeah go have one. Might get some of the rage out of you.

Kate   Alright whatever. Have fun when your dad comes home and decides to scream at you. Picking up next week. Need a tenner from you.

Sam   Fine I'll get it to you.

. . .

Pete   I feel like I'm not achieving my full potential.

Kate   Yeah wanking thirteen times a day will probably have that effect.

Pete   I mean it though.

Sam   What?

Pete   I don't know what to do. Need something to pass the time. Need some money.

Sam   Get a job.

Pete   Oh aye I'll just get a job then that easy is it?

Sam   I have.

Kate   Yeah good job that one and all isn't it? How's that promotion coming in the newsagent's?

Sam   Better than nothing. More than you're doing isn't it?

Kate   What?

Sam   Said was more than you're doing.

Kate   What with?

Pete   Jobs and work and that.

Kate   Not thought about that.

Pete   Oh yeah?

Kate   No. Leave town first and then think about all that.

Sam   Think you probably need work to leave.

Kate   No work about though is there?

Pete   Must be something? Supermarket?

Kate   Better than that.

Pete   Oh yeah?

Kate   Didn't go to school do a load of shite exams and jump through a load of hoops to work in a supermarket did we?

Pete   Dunno. Some people think it's alright.

Kate   Not us.

Pete   Supermarket's not hiring anyway. Asked there. Would have been perfect. Me and that girl on the meat counter. Sausages everywhere.

Kate   Sausages? What is it with you and fucking sausages?

Pete   Alright just joking. But seriously. Bit stuck aren't we. Thinking about it.

Kate   Yeah.

Pete   I think I'd like to be a fireman. I was very inspired when they put out my house that time.

Sam   What you?

Pete   Yeah. Be amazing that.

Kate   You'd be shite at it.

Pete   Bollocks would I.

Kate   Soft as shit. Scared of the dark aren't you?

Pete   So?

Kate   So if you're scared of the dark how're you going to leg it in a fire?

Sam   Wouldn't be dark.

Kate   Know what I meant.

Pete   Think I would be shite at it?

Kate   Yeah.

Pete   Oh. Well that's that dream gone.

Sam   Can't be a fireman round here anyway.

Pete   Why not?

Sam   No fire station is there?

Pete   Oh is there not? Thought there was one in every town.

Kate   Not this one.

Pete   Where'd they come from then?

Sam   Miles away I think.

Pete   That's mad isn't it? Imagine if my house had burned down and all because they took ages to get there? Wouldn't be my fault then would it?

Kate   Well yeah.

Pete   Yeah I guess. Oh well. This is weird isn't it?

Sam   What is?

Pete   Another year's nearly gone. Felt like we left school only a few minutes ago. No idea what to do with jobs and that. But maybe I don't care. Thinking about it. I don't think I care. Because I think I just want to be a dad.

Sam   A what?

Pete   A dad.

Kate   Be a dad?

Pete   Yeah just said that. Think that's all I want to be really. My brother's baby. I can't stop thinking about him. Keep looking at him when he's asleep. Little baby lying there. Just want to pick him up. Carry him about for a bit. But I don't do that. Because if I wake him up my brother explodes. And that's not worth the punches. So I just look at him sleeping. Do that every night. See his little chest going up and down. Imagine what he's thinking. Try and work out what pictures are inside his head. What I look like in his tiny memories. Can't. Can't think about anything else but that.

. . .

Sam   Where did you get it from?

Kate   Some bloke at the pub.

Pete   Who's that then?

Kate   Some bloke in the Oak. Dunno. Just hung about outside a bit. Only wanted some weed but he was like weed's boring have some ketamine.

Sam   Sounds legit.

Kate   Said it was decent.

Pete   Who?

Kate   Who what?

Pete   Who was it then?

Kate   Dunno some bloke.

Pete   Did he have one eye?

Kate   Don't know didn't notice.

Pete   Didn't notice?

Kate   Dunno.

Pete   You didn't notice if the bloke you were talking to had one eye?

Kate   Well one eye was closed.

Sam   I know him. Comes in the shop. Keep thinking he's winking at me but then it just stays shut.

Pete   Nah he's not winking at you. He's only got one eye. Because you can't wink if you haven't got an eye to wink.

Kate   How'd you know?

Pete   What? Well because the eye isn't there for like your eyelid to close over then –

Kate   Didn't mean that did I? Meant how did you know him.

Pete   Oh right because I do. Brother knows him. Tell you something and all right.

Kate   What?

Pete   That bloke.

Kate   What about him?

Pete   With the one eye right?

Kate   Yeah?

Pete   His nickname.

Kate   What about it?

Pete   Is One-eye Steve.

Sam   Catchy that.

Pete   Because he's only got one eye that's why he's called –

Sam   Yeah got that one.

Pete   Right yeah my brother said he lost his eye because someone punched him in the head once and his eye fell out and the bloke that punched him just legged it right but Steve knew the bloke's cousin or something so he was like I'll sort him next week I know where he lives or something with his eye like hanging out of his face right –

Kate   Bullshit.

Pete   Nah nah true that. Apparently he was so drunk he just like pushed it back in and kept drinking and everyone was like Steve mate your eye doesn't look too good there mate and he was like I'm fine just a scratch mate and then someone was like doesn't look like a scratch Steve mate because your eye's not where it should be there. He wasn't bothered right just kept drinking and went home but then apparently right he woke up the next morning and it was still giving him grief so he just pulled it out right. And then right he posted it to the bloke who punched him with a note saying I've got my eye on you. Bet the bloke shat himself then. One-eye Steve right there. Mad that isn't it? Now he's a drug dealer so seems like he's got a good hold on his life and is really making all the right decisions right?

Kate   Talk such shite you.

Pete   Do I bollocks? About as much as you. Difference is that everything I say is true. Could write a book.

Sam   What about?

Pete   This town. All the stories that come out of it. Best-seller that. Make a fortune. Read them to my kids at bedtime.

Kate   Could do that if you could spell or read.

Sam   Or write.

Pete   I can write can't I? Wrote that exam ages ago didn't I?

Sam   How did that go?

Pete   I can spell a bit and all.

Kate   You can that's right.

Pete   Exactly.

Kate   Just that if you get to a word that's longer than three letters then that's where things fall apart a bit don't they?

Pete   Can spell a word more than three letters can't I? Name's got six hasn't it?

Sam   What Pete?

Pete   Yeah.

Kate   That's four you fucking idiot.

Pete   Meant Peter didn't I?

Sam   And that's five.

Pete   Ah fuck off that's not the point is it? Point is I've got stories. And people love a story don't they?

Sam   Some do.

Kate   Not about this place.

Pete   Why's that then?

Kate   No one cares about towns surrounded by fields do they? Or the people inside them. Like us. No one's interested in the towns that sit like islands in the middle of fields. Never have been. Never will be.

. . .

Kate   Why's all your stuff all over the place?

Pete   Brother lobbed it out the house.

Kate   Why?

Pete   Came back pissed and thought I'd hidden the TV remote.

Kate   So he chucked all your gear out?

Pete   It's alright I don't mind.

Kate   And now you're standing out here?

Pete   Yeah he locked me out. I'm freezing. What you doing here anyway?

Kate   Dad was coughing. Didn't want to listen to it any more. Come for a walk?

Pete   Middle of the night.

Kate   So?

Pete   Can't anyway.

Kate   Why not?

Pete   Brother said I have to stand here.

Kate   What?

Pete   I have to stand here and if I move he'll kick my head in.

Kate   Your brother mate.

Pete   Prick isn't he?

Kate   All because he thinks you hid a TV remote.

Pete   Yeah well I did hide it and all.

Kate   Why?

Pete   Keeps having a go at me about not bringing any money home.

Kate   What's that got to do with him?

Pete   Says I have to pay rent.

Kate   It's your house too isn't it?

Pete   I know but he won't shut up about it. Going to see about getting on Jobseekers and that. Which makes me feel a bit empty. Don't know why. It shouldn't should it? There to help isn't it? Not to make you feel like you're not worth anything.

Kate   So you're just going to give your brother your dole money?

Pete   Dunno what else to do.

Kate   Tell him to fuck off.

Pete   And get the shit kicked out of me again? I'm good for that cheers. You should get on and all. If he comes back and you're here he'll kick off. You really need to stop throwing up on his car you know?

Kate   Can't help it. Ugliest car I've ever seen. Have to throw up on it.

Pete   He really hates you you know.

Kate   Yeah I know. Don't care about that. Just care about getting out of here.

Pete   Yeah maybe.

Kate   Maybe? Definitely. My dad. Sam's dad. Your brother. That's not right is it?

Pete   No guess not.

Kate   Not fair.

Pete   I know but –

Kate   But what?

Pete   I'm just worried about it is all.

Kate   Worried about what? We'll be fine.

Pete   No not us. My brother's kid. Feels like I need to look after it. You know? Because. Because I don't think my brother knows anything about it.

Kate   About what?

Pete   About love.

. . .

Pete   I forgot.

Kate   Fucksake man one thing I asked you to get. What did I say? Pete get papers because you can't smoke a joint without papers and I'm getting everything else aren't I? One thing. One fucking thing.

Pete   Alright calm down –

Kate   Go to the shop for us.

Sam   Closed isn't it?

Kate   Useless you. Don't know why I hang about with you.

Pete   Because you've got no other mates.

Kate   Doesn't matter anyway. I nicked some painkillers so can get high off them.

Sam   Who off?

Kate   My dad who'd you think?

Sam   Doesn't he need them?

Kate   Got loads. And I need them more. Want one?

Sam   Stick to cider.

Kate   Suit yourself. You?

Pete   Alright why not. What they do?

Kate   Dunno. Get you high I think.

Pete   That's top. And I've got a bit of a headache and all so two birds one stone hey? They'll knock a headache out won't they?

Sam   Yeah probably if they're meant for what her dad's got.

Kate   Shut up saying that about my dad.

Sam   Alright just saying –

Kate   Well don't alright he's fine.

Sam   Don't think he is that fine really though?

Kate   Told you shut up about it.

Sam   Never talk about it.

Kate   Why'd I need to talk about it?

Sam   Don't know. Just think you should. Reckon you should be ready for it or something.

Kate   Ready for what?

Sam   When he goes.

Pete   Yeah that'll be a shit day won't it?

Kate   What day?

Pete   Coming home drunk like you always are and finding your dad dead. I mean. That'd kill the buzz a bit wouldn't it?

Kate   Won't happen.

Pete   I think it might there mate.

Kate   Won't.

Pete   I've got an idea for you.

Kate   What's that?

Pete   You should get a hamster or something.

Kate   Why?

Pete   Because they don't last very long do they?

Sam   So?

Pete   So it'll die and then you can practise doing some grieving for when your dad goes.

Sam   Is that the same thing?

Pete   Close enough. I can get you one though.

Kate   I don't want –

Pete   My brother's mate sells them.

Sam   What?

Pete   He's got a little shop in his front room.

Sam   What shop?

Pete   Sells all sorts. Rodents and that though is what he specialises in. He loves it. Breeds them and sells them. Cheap and all. Fiver or something. Fiver for a little hamster that's a good deal isn't it? If you have a tenner you could buy two. And that is maths.

Sam   Genius.

Pete   If you had a twenty you could buy five.

Sam   Jesus.

Pete   But give me a shout anyway.

Kate   Yeah I'm alright for that thanks.

Pete   Fair enough. You?

Sam   I'm good for a rodent.

Pete   Alright no worries I'm not bothered at least that means I don't have to go round his house because it stinks.

Sam   Really why's that then?

Pete   Yeah because he's got a load of rodents shitting all – Oh you were being sarcastic. You're hard.

Kate   Pass that.

Pete   Make it last like. Only got the one.

Kate   What?

Pete   All I could find in the house.

Kate   Fucksake. One can?

Pete   Not much I can do about it.

Kate   Last us a while isn't it?

Sam   Took a load of painkillers didn't you?

Kate   Fuck-all point if you've got nothing to come up on is there? All be asleep.

Pete   Fine by me I would love a sleep. Not here though. Freeze to death wouldn't you. Then we'd be dead. Which wouldn't be ideal. Oh speaking of rodents right. Bought that girl a mouse the other day. Wasn't into it still.

Sam   Who?

Pete   Girl in the supermarket.

Kate   Still trying with that?

Pete   Yeah.

Kate   How long's that been?

Pete   Dunno. Year and a half or something?

Kate   Not think you should probably leave it there?

Pete   Nah I'll keep trying. Annoying she didn't like the mouse though.

Sam   Funny that.

Pete   Nah wasn't a manky one.

Sam   Did she mention it before?

Pete   Mention what?

Sam   Liking mice.

Pete   No.

Kate   So why'd you buy her one?

Pete   Because they're cute and that. Just a present like. A token of my love for her.

Kate   You're not in love with her.

Pete   I am. That's all I am. I love her OK? I'm in love. I'm literally in love with her. I want to make love to her. Very slowly. Very gently.

Sam   Gross.

Pete   By candlelight.

Kate   Fucking candles. What is it with him and candles? Why the candles? What're the candles all about?

Pete   What people do isn't it?

Kate   No.

Pete   Have you?

Kate   No.

Pete   Ah because you've not been romanced. Me right. I'm romantic. So I'm all over the candles and that shite. Yeah? Seventeen now. Time to stop being kiddies with this love shite. Step it all up.

Kate   Mice and candles then?

Sam   Better than sausages.

Kate   That's true.

Pete   Anyway. Got a mouse now. Don't want it. Just going to let it go. Give it its freedom. Be alright that. Tell you something.

Sam   What?

Pete   I don't think it was the mouse really.

Kate   No?

Pete   I think it was because I followed her home.

Kate   Yeah that'll do it.

Sam   You followed her?

Pete   Yeah. Not like directly behind her like. Just like. Few metres behind.

Sam   Yeah that doesn't make it creepy then.

Pete   Didn't mean to do that did I? Just didn't. Didn't know what to say so just followed her. Didn't want to follow her. Wanted to talk to her. But. Couldn't. Always the way isn't it that?

Sam   What is?

Pete   You just lie about thinking about what you could say. All these amazing things in your head. Saying them inside your own mind. Then when it comes to it everything sounds wrong and you can't even speak. What's that about then?

Sam   Dunno.

Pete   Me either. You ever get that?

Sam   I guess.

Pete   Yeah. Don't get that. Don't think I'll ever be able to not do that. Just be me. Thinking stuff. And that's all it is isn't it? Life's just thinking. Then you die. And that's all it is. Right? That's all. All it is. Just thinking about doing and saying things. And some people can. But I can't. And that's. That's not good is it? I mean. To just dream and never actually do. That's. Why can't I do that? Jesus these painkillers are something weird aren't they? What am I talking about? Feels like I could float. Float and drift. Drift to the horizon and see what's after it.

. . .

Sam   It's not that bad.

Kate   Doesn't look it. Fuck happened?

Sam   Dad came back drunk and smacked me. It's alright. Just a black eye is all.

Kate   Is all?

Sam   Was shouting. Just let him hit me. Easier that way. Sister woke up because of the noise. He just passed out and I spent the rest of the night trying to get her back to sleep.

Kate   Call the police?

Sam   What they going to do?

Kate   Put him away.

Sam   Then what?

Kate   What?

Sam   What I do then? Dad inside and Mum not interested in coming back. Me and my sister doing what? She'll get taken in somewhere and I'll have nowhere to stay. Rather put up with this.

Kate   I wouldn't.

Sam   No choice have I?

Kate   Smack him back?

Sam   Wish I could. Got this idea anyway.

Kate   What's that?

Sam   Saved up some from the shop. Next year when I'm eighteen going to rent a little flat in town. Just live there with my sister.

Kate   Don't do that.

Sam   Why not?

Kate   Because it's not your problem.

Sam   It is though isn't it?

Kate   Don't think so. Tell you something.

Sam   What's that?

Kate   Went out in my dad's car last night.

Sam   Did you?

Kate   Yeah. Practising. It's a piece of piss. Drove it about town then the ring road. Just went round and round. Was amazing. Orbited the town like I was in a spaceship or something. Town on my left. Horizon on my right. Was amazing. Driving about. Never felt so free. Just pick a direction and we're gone.

Sam   That easy is it?

Kate   You know if you climb up the swings and sit on the bar at the top you can see the horizon through the little gap in the trees. Just a curved line. That's all it is. Just a curved line resting on top of the earth. But looking at it. Looks fragile. Like it could just move away. Leaving a space behind. And I reckon if we're not careful that's where we're going to end up. So fuck your dad and come with me.

Sam   Can't do that though.

Kate   Why not?

Sam   Because my little sister needs protecting. Don't want to leave her alone. Weird this isn't it? Being here. Feeling the world spinning around me. Feels like the town's not letting us go. Even if I did want to escape. I don't think I ever could.

. . .

Pete   Said I had to go back every two weeks.

Kate   How long's that take?

Pete   Ages. And costs about as much.

Sam   How much is it?

Pete   Just under sixty quid. Gave up talking to them because worked out the train would cost too much to actually bother going to pick it up. And there's no buses to the station any more so that's the end of that then. Just hung up the phone.

Kate   Dunno why you even bothered with it.

Pete   Keep my brother happy. Or whatever he thinks that is.

Sam   Nothing where he works?

Pete   He hasn't got one either has he?

Sam   What happened?

Pete   Factory closed down didn't it?

Sam   Didn't notice that happening. Can't he drive you then?

Pete   He won't do that would he?

Sam   He'll have to go now too right? Not having a job?

Pete   He won't. Says people on the dole are scum.

Sam   But he wants you on it?

Pete   Yeah.

Kate   Your brother's a dickhead.

Pete   I know.

Sam   It's stupid you can't get on the dole anyway because of geography isn't it?

Pete   Guess so. If I had a car I could drive there. But don't have one so can't. And also don't know how to drive. You know what I think what would really help me out here is some fucking public transport.

Kate   Sat on a bus that smells of piss taking you to sign on. Sounds like a laugh.

Pete   What you saying then?

Kate   Told you.

Pete   Oh right this about you and your dad's car again. She told you about that?

Kate   Yeah.

Pete   Do you believe her?

Kate   Why would I lie?

Pete   Dunno just seems a bit funny is all.

Kate   Funny?

Pete   Drunk all the time aren't you? If you got in a car you'd crash it into someone's nan or something. Like straight away. Just get in turn the key put your foot down and then go oh shite I've killed a nan.

Kate   Why would I lie about it? Not just doing this for me. For all of us. Keep dreaming about it?

Pete   What driving your dad's shit old car?

Kate   Just driving. Getting off a road that doesn't just go in circles. One that's a straight line that actually leads somewhere else. Out past the horizon. And then the next one. Don't even know what I want to do. But just know I've got do that you know?

Pete   Make me laugh you.

Kate   Why?

Pete   Talking like that.

Kate   Like what?

Pete   Like it's that easy.

Kate   What she said.

Pete   She's right then.

Kate   Why's it not?

Pete   Because got no money for a start. And you know you need that to make a car literally move don't you? And anyway what am I going to do outside of this town? Can't do anything here. Thick as shit aren't I? So what's the point not being able to do something anywhere else. All I want to do is just find somebody that doesn't think I stink and have a nice big family and –

Kate   Talking about this again?

Pete   Nothing wrong with it is there?

Kate   Fucking boring isn't it? That all you want?

Pete   Hundred million per cent yes.

Kate   Well then do all that somewhere else. Might find someone you don't have to follow about and buy fucking mice for. And who actually talks to you.

Pete   She is talking to me now.

Sam   Is she?

Pete   Yeah.

Sam   What she say?

Pete   Hello.

Sam   What else?

Pete   Bye.

Sam   Making progress then?

Pete   Ah better than nothing isn't it? And anyway I'm going to ask her out now. Nothing to lose hey? Worst thing that happens? I stay like this. Best thing. She says yes. And I'm like right then date night let's do this. And I met up with her. And I'm all like alright what's up and she's like oh my God every-thing I've heard about you is true you are a legend and I'm like yeah I know I'm very very very very special and then we walk hand in hand in the moonlight and then just like fall in love. By candlelight. And then shag each other. Have thirty kids.

Sam   In one go?

Pete   Yeah. Is that possible?

Sam   Have a guess.

Pete   No?

Sam   No spot on.

Kate   Don't ask her.

Pete   Why not?

Kate   Because she'll say no.

Pete   Why?

Kate   Why? Because you look like a fish mate.

Pete   Well that's –

Kate   And you've been stalking her for a year and a half. She's not going to want to go out with a sex pest is she mate?

Pete   Alright yeah but worth a try isn't it?

Sam   Ask her.

Pete   Yeah?

Sam   Yeah do it so I don't have to listen to you talk about it any more.

Pete   Yeah fuck it. I will.

Kate   Don't.

Sam   Why can't he?

Kate   Been years hasn't it? She's not interested. And she's boring as shit anyway. Working in a supermarket? Sounds like a catch.

Pete   Alright easy how'd you know what she's like?

Kate   Seen her in there. Just plods about. Looks dull as anything. Looks like a ghost. Just be shagging a ghost. Bet she doesn't even drink and all.

Pete   That is it then? You looked at her and decided she's boring.

Kate   Yeah. Trust me.

Pete   What and she should be more like you?

Kate   What's that mean?

Pete   Pissed all the time.

Kate   Fun isn't it?

Pete   Oh right yeah? Like the other night fun?

Kate   That was funny.

Sam   What's that?

Pete   Want me to tell her?

Sam   What about?

Pete   Other night right. I'm in bed. Just hanging out with my own thoughts and that.

Kate   Few candles set up.

Pete   And hear this sound from outside like someone laughing but trying not to you know. And then look and it's her. Steaming. Off her tits right. Jumping up and down on my brother's car.

Sam   On your own?

Kate   Yeah.

Pete   And I'm like this isn't good so leg it down and push her off the car just as my brother comes out the house in his pants and he's raging right. Absolute pissing mad.

Sam   Did he see you on the car?

Pete   Nah thank God but he does see her lying in the drive with a bottle of vodka –

Kate   Gin.

Pete   Right gin. Sorry because that's important. And anyway my brother screaming for her to piss off and she stands up and just screams. Didn't you?

Kate   Think so can't remember.

Pete   Just screams so loud that all the neighbours wake up and my little nephew wakes up and they're all shouting now and my brother is in his pants just screaming at her and she wobbles a bit and drops the vodka –

Kate   Gin.

Pete   Fucksake. Gin. Whatever. Drops the gin. Gin everywhere. Then right. Then she just starts licking it up. Glass and all. Blood in her mouth. Then gets up. Throws up on his car and walks off and my brother's like the absolute state of your mates to me.

Kate   Funny that right?

Sam   Dunno.

Kate   What?

Sam   Not. Not really.

Kate   No?

Sam   No.

Kate   Why not?

Sam   Dunno. Just. Everyone see you?

Kate   Wasn't many.

Sam   Still though. Be talking about you now.

Kate   So?

Sam   Just think.

Kate   What?

Sam   Nothing doesn't matter.

Kate   Nothing?

Sam   Yeah. It's fine. Hope you're alright and that.

Kate   I'm alright yeah.

Sam   That's good then.

Kate   Is it?

Sam   Yeah.

Kate   What?

Sam   Nothing.

Kate   Tell me –

Sam   Said it's nothing. It's alright. Everything's alright.

. . .

Kate   Think I'm a fuck-up don't you?

Sam   No.

Kate   I'm not.

Sam   I know. I don't think that.

Kate   Why's it feel like that then?

Sam   Wasn't anything to do with you. Just. Dunno.

Kate   Need to drink more you. Loosen up.

Sam   Yeah maybe.

Kate   Mean it.

Sam   Can I ask you something?

Kate   Anything.

Sam   You feel like you're seventeen?

Kate   What?

Sam   You feel like you are?

Kate   Dunno. Not thought about it. Guess so. Do you?

Sam   No.

Kate   No?

Sam   Feel like I'm old. Feel like I've been living for longer than I ever should have. And that's weird because it feels like we were all fifteen about half an hour ago. You know?

Kate   Guess so.

Sam   What we doing Kate? Feels like we're drifting doesn't it? Just drinking and drifting. All this. Doesn't feel like the world exists beyond the ring road does it?

Kate   It does.

Sam   Yeah?

Kate   Can see it when you're driving round and round. It's there. I promise.

Sam   Went out there the other night.

Kate   Where to?

Sam   Edge of town. Just walked about. Dad passed out. TV on. Looked at him for a bit then thought about my sister. Picked her up and carried her out. Just carried her. Walked to the edge of town. Holding her. Got to the ring road. Thought about crossing it then out into the fields. Just keep walking. Keep walking until we got to the sea. Just to look at a horizon that was blue instead of green and brown. That's all I wanted. But got to the edge of the road and couldn't take one step further. Don't know why. Like my feet were stuck to the town. Just couldn't move. Felt like a ghost. Just empty. Couldn't take another step forward. So just turned around and went home. Put my sister back to bed. Went downstairs. Sat watching my dad's chest rise and fall. Think I could see the air going in and out of his mouth illuminated by the light of the TV. Had this thought that I could just stab him in the throat. Over and over again. Watch the blood fall out. Then I would get my sister again and walk back to the ring road and be able to cross it. But I didn't do that. I just went to bed and got up the next morning and made my sister her breakfast and walked her to school. Another year's nearly gone. Nearly an adult. A horizon for you to walk into. No idea about any of that. Feels like I've been old for years. Can I tell you something else and all?

Kate   What?

Sam   Think I've reached my horizon you know? And it's the ring road.

. . .

Pete   One-eye Steve kicked me in the balls.

Kate   Why?

Pete   Wanted to buy some ketamine. Didn't have enough money. Said I'd write him a cheque. He didn't like that. So he kicked me in the balls.

Sam   You've got a cheque book?

Pete   How hard do you need to be kicked for your balls to not work at making kids any more?

Kate   Dunno not got any.

Pete   Right yeah. But. A guess.

Kate   No idea. Hard.

Pete   It was hard. Felt like my balls were going to come out my mouth. Just hang there so I could look at them and see how useless they probably are. Think that's my chances of kids gone.

Kate   That might be good for the world.

Pete   Fuck off. The one hope I've got left isn't it?

Sam   What?

Pete   My balls. If they don't work then I've got no idea have I? What am I then? Having a load of kids is my one plan isn't it? If that's gone then I've got nothing. Just me. A bloke called Pete. That's fucking it.

Sam   You're in a good mood.

Pete   Guess so.

Sam   What happened to all that massive family full of hope stuff?

Pete   Yeah still clinging on to that if my balls work.

Sam   You'll be alright.

Pete   Really starting to think I won't there mate. I mean how long have I lived for? Feels like forever. How long?

Sam   What you want me to say it?

Pete   Yeah. Tell me.

Sam   Eighteen years now.

Pete   Eighteen years I lived in this town? So I'm eighteen in age now then?

Sam   That's maths.

Pete   Jesus I'm not eighteen am I? What have I done? Nothing. Have I shagged anyone? Have I? Tell me?

Sam   You want me to –

Pete   Yeah.

Sam   No?

Pete   No I haven't. Not even kissed anyone. Since your nan mate. Fucking hell can't be can it? I think it is. And that was like years and years ago. Jesus. What have I been doing?

Kate   Giving mice to women.

Pete   Mean it. Jokes aside and all that? What the fuck am I doing?

Kate   Calm down.

Pete   I'm not calming down. Think I'm having a breakdown.

Kate   What right now?

Pete   Yeah.

Kate   Seem like you're the same as normal.

Pete   I'm not. My mind. Inside of here. My stupid head. It's full-on going mad.

Kate   Sure it's not all the speed you just took?

Pete   No. Well. Partly. But that's only opening my eyes and mind to how completely fucked I am. What are we going to do?

Kate   Been telling you.

Pete   Right yeah I don't think just leaving in your dad's stolen car is really the answer to all our problems is it?

Kate   Why not?

Pete   Because it's stupid.

Kate   Why?

Pete   Because it is.

Kate   That it?

Pete   That's it what?

Kate   Not going to tell me why it's stupid?

Pete   Because it's not going to happen ever.

Kate   Why not?

Pete   Because I don't believe you. Going out in your dad's car. Talking nonsense mate.

Kate   Not making it up. Ask her.

Sam   What?

Kate   Not making it up am I?

Sam   I don't know.

Kate   What?

Sam   Never seen you driving it.

Kate   What?

Sam   Just saying.

Kate   Saying what? Both don't believe me?

Pete   No. Not at all. My head. Just spinning and spinning.

Kate   Be alright calm –

Pete   I don't think I will Kate. I really don't. Feel so empty. Can't do anything. Can't even ask a girl out. Fuck me. I'm meant to be an adult aren't I? That's what they tell you? Don't they?

Kate   I guess.

Pete   Then why do I feel like a kid? Eighteen-year-old kid?
Thing is though that kids are meant to bounce when they fall
over aren't they? But me. I feel like a kid who if they fell over
would shatter into a million pieces.

. . .

Kate   You can't live there.

Sam   Why not? It's cheap.

Kate   Because it's a shithole.

Sam   Better than nothing.

Kate   Walls are more mould than paint.

Sam   All I can afford isn't it?

Kate   Put our money together and get a place somewhere
else?

Sam   You've got no money.

Kate   I know but can get some.

Sam   Yeah? Where from?

Kate   You can't live there.

Sam   Look at my face Kate.

Kate   What?

Sam   See those bruises?

Kate   Yeah.

Sam   Now tell me I can't live there.

Kate   I'm not going to let you do this.

Sam   Why not?

Kate   Move into a shitty flat in the middle of the town you
grew up in. I'd do anything to not have you do that. I'd stab
your dad for you. Just say the word. I would.

Sam   Don't be stupid.

Kate   I'm not. If you won't let me do that then the only other thing to do is come with me. Because thinking about you sitting in that flat. Eighteen watching the paint dissolve off the walls in front of you. That's not going to keep your sister safe you know? That's not. And I'm not letting you do that. Just come with me. Somewhere else. Anywhere and –

Sam   You seen Pete?

Kate   Don't change the subject mate I'm –

Sam   Have you seen Pete?

Kate   You can't live –

Sam   You seen him?

Kate   No.

Sam   Been two weeks.

Kate   Tried calling. Went round. Anyway –

Sam   Nothing?

Kate   No?

Sam   At all?

Kate   Nothing. Sure he'll be alright. Mean it Sam. Get in a car with me. I'll take you somewhere where you don't have to worry any more. Alright? Please. For me. For yourself.

. . .

Kate   Where you been then? Hiding?

Pete   I guess. Worried about me or something?

Kate   No. What you been doing?

Pete   Just lying in bed. Couldn't get out.

Kate   At all.

Pete   No. Thought about it every morning and then just couldn't. Like I was stuck inside it. Just listening to my brother shout at his kid. Horrible that. Want to pick it up and run away with it you know? Sorry for having a freak-out like.

Kate   It's alright happens. Sam does it all the time.

Pete   She said yes by the way.

Kate   Who?

Pete   Asked that girl out?

Kate   Thought you couldn't get out of bed?

Pete   This morning. Just was like. Fuck it. Not getting like that ever again. Go mental like that. Lying about in bed. Eighteen. Need to do something. Anything. So just asked. And she said yes. Know you think I'm being a dick but I really do like her you know? Hope she doesn't think I'm a bellend. You seen that flat Sam wants to move into?

Kate   Yeah.

Pete   Might be good for her.

Kate   You reckon?

Pete   Dunno. Might be. Don't you?

Kate   No.

Pete   Why not?

Kate   Because it looks like the place you would go to live in when you want to be forgotten. And I'm not letting that happen.

. . .

Kate   So I drove it here.

Pete   Bollocks you did.

Kate   Don't believe me go look.

Pete   Where is it?

Kate   Just over there mate.

Sam   You drunk?

Kate   No.

Sam   High?

Kate   No. Told you. Think I'm joking or something?

Sam   No it's just –

Kate   What?

Sam   Can't just –

Kate   Just what?

Sam   Can't just leave.

Kate   Why not?

Sam   Because of everything here.

Kate   And what's that? What's here? That shitty flat?

Sam   Yeah that and my family and –

Kate   Family? Some families we've got right? Dad who kicks the shit out of you and a brother who can't stand the sight of you. Why'd you want to stay with that?

Sam   Not that it's just –

Kate   Then what is it then? Your sister? Worried about her? Just an excuse that.

Sam   Excuse for what?

Kate   For not being brave enough to do anything about your own life. Told you so many times right. It's not your fucking problem. And neither is your brother's kid to you. It's not yours mate is it?

Pete   I know but –

Kate   But what? What you going to do? Both of you? Just hang about here worrying about them until they can worry about themselves? Then what'll you have then? Nearly thirty in the same town going what the fuck have I done? That's no way to live is it? Towns like these are for leaving. And then coming back to sometimes to remind yourself why you left.

Sam   Said I can't.

Kate And I said that you don't because you're scared.

Sam Not scared.

Kate What then?

Sam Have to be here.

Kate Then what's the point then? Tell me that.

Pete Of what?

Kate Of existing.

Pete Listen to you.

Kate What?

Pete Talking like that. Existing. Are existing aren't we?

Kate Barely. All you both do is moan. Daydream about stabbing your dad. That's healthy isn't it mate?

Sam Alright just –

Kate Why don't you? Just go stab him. Go on. Then everything would be alright wouldn't it?

Sam Alright just –

Kate Just what?

Sam Why don't you go then?

Kate What?

Sam Go by yourself. If you want to so much. Why'd you need us?

Kate Because I'm not doing this for me. I'm doing this for us all. I need you to come with me because I couldn't live with the thought that you both are living like you are right now. You in that shitty flat and you getting the shit kicked out of you by your brother and going after some girl that you don't even like.

Pete She didn't turn up anyway.

Kate No?

Pete   No.

Kate   Well there you go. Haven't even got that any more. Got nothing now have you? Like everyone in this town.

Pete   Jesus.

Kate   What?

Pete   No wonder we don't go to the pub.

Kate   What?

Pete   Talking like that you'll. Get your head kicked in.

Kate   Why's that then?

Sam   Because there's a lot of people who think you're talking shite. There's a load of people out there who'd probably be a bit fed up or something talking like that. About their hometown. Alright? And what about your dad?

Kate   What about him?

Sam   How he would feel? Left alone.

Kate   Not my problem is it?

Sam   No?

Kate   No it's not alright.

Sam   Why's that then?

Kate   Because fuck him that's why.

Pete   What?

Kate   Not fair is it?

Pete   Don't choose to get sick do you?

Kate   Not him. Me.

Sam   What?

Kate   Not fair on me.

Pete   I know but –

Kate   They took his carer away you know?

Pete   What? Why?

Kate   Don't fucking know do I? To save some money?
Or something? Just cut them like they've cut everything else.
Weeks ago. And now no one comes round. And it's all me.
I have to go pick up his pills and bring them home. I have
to feed him. I have to take him to the toilet. That's my job?
To clean up his shit and piss and listen to his bones slowly
rotting? Fuck that thanks. That's not what I should be doing.
He should be properly looked after. And the worst thing is
right. You want to know the worst thing? I think I hate him.

Pete   Do you?

Kate   For being sick. Think I really hate him.

Pete   That's –

Kate   And not because of what he's got. Just because of
what it does to me. And if I say that to anyone people will just
think I'm scum won't they?

Pete   Suppose.

Kate   But I don't think I care you know? Think I'm scum.
I don't give a shit. Because I deserve something better than
this right? Doesn't everyone? And this town. Inside this dying
town. This won't ever give us what we deserve. I mean. Look
at you.

Sam   What?

Kate   It's like everything's fallen out of you. And you. Just
two ghosts. Empty. And I can't look at you like this any more.
I know you both think I'm full of shit. But I'll be your guide
out of here. Mean it. Don't think either of you know it but
I'm both of yours guardian angel. Just one driving my dying
dad's shitty old car. We're bigger than this. We're bigger than
this town. And we're bigger than a horizon that's going to
leave us behind if we don't fucking do something about it.
All that bravery inside of you. I know it's there somewhere.

Just too scared to use it. What you want to do to your dad. How you would love to smack him back but can't.

Sam   Shut up alright –

Kate   Why? Because I'm right.

Sam   No because –

Kate   Because what? You couldn't. It's all gone from you. That fight. It's gone.

Sam   It's not –

Kate   It has.

Sam   It hasn't.

Kate   Prove it then.

Sam   What?

Kate   Smack me. Go on. I don't mind.

Sam   What?

Kate   Punch me then. Prove it.

Sam   Don't –

Kate   Don't what?

Sam   Don't do –

Kate   Do what? I don't mind. Prove to me there's something left in you. That your dad hasn't taken it out of you.

Pete   Well this is fun.

Kate   You and all. Smack me if you want.

Pete   I'm alright thanks.

Sam   How drunk are you?

Kate   Not had a drop. Go on. Hit me. Show me you've still got something inside of you?

Sam   I don't need to prove –

Kate   Show me then.

Sam   This is –

Kate   Show me. What you going to do? Work in a newsagent's until your sister can look after herself? Sounds good doesn't it?

Sam   Have to –

Kate   No you don't. You're scared because you're empty so hit me. Show me something.

Sam   I'm not –

Kate   Go on.

Sam   Stop it.

Kate   Go on. Hit me.

Sam   No.

Kate   Hit me.

Sam   Not going –

Kate   Do it. Come on. Tell her.

Pete   Tell her what –

Kate   To hit me.

Sam   I'm not –

Kate   Smack me.

Sam   No.

Kate   Do it.

Sam   No.

Kate   Hit me.

Sam   Shut –

Kate   Hit me.

Sam   Calm down alright I'm not –

Kate   Hit me come on.

Sam   I'm not going to –

Kate   Hit me come on.

Sam   I'm not –

Kate   Do it.

Sam   No.

Kate   Do it.

Sam   No.

Kate   Fucking hit –

Sam   I'm not going –

Kate   Hit me.

Sam   Just –

Kate   Smack me in the face go on I want you to.

Sam   Said I –

Kate   Do it do it do it –

Sam   Stop –

Kate   Do it do it do it do it hit me alright hit me like your dad likes to hit you and your little sister –

Sam *punches* **Kate** *in the face. Hard.*

Pete   Fucking hell –

Kate   Fuck. Yes mate. That's it. That's the way. Yes mate. That's what I wanted. Fucking hell that felt alright.

Pete   Jesus.

Kate   Am I bleeding?

Pete   A bit yeah –

Kate   Thank you mate.

Pete   With the ring and all.

Kate Oh yeah could have taken that off couldn't you mate? That's not bad at all. That's what I needed. Want a go?

Pete I'm alright –

Kate See?

Sam See what?

Kate What friends are for isn't it?

Pete What punching each other?

Kate Yeah that and the rest. And all of it. Listen to me Sam. Listen to me right now. You listening? I'm going to tell you something alright. I'll tell you something?

Sam What?

Kate I love you alright? I love you so much it hurts. And what's going on with you and your dad and your little sister is not for you to fix alright? You stay here you'll end up just like your dad you know? Full of rage and shouting at nothing. So look at me. Right into my eyes and see that I'm doing this because I love you more than anyone ever could and I can't think about anything but that. I can't think about leaving without you because he's always been right since he said it years and years ago. Home is wherever you both are. It isn't bricks and parks and roads and shops. It's wherever we are together. Alright? The blood running down the side of my face. That belongs to you. And I love you even more for doing that. You know? Because it shows you're not a ghost. You're real. And I think I love you so much I could explode. I could. I could burst how much I love you both. I feel like I could just fill up. Just fill up till I'm sick. Till I'm sick with it. Till I just throw up all the love out of my mouth and it would just be us in it all. Swimming in it. Swimming in all that love that's around us. Just me and you and you as little islands in the middle of it. And I just think we should get in that car right now and go somewhere. Away from your dad and your brother and everything else. Alright? Let's go. Anywhere. I don't care. Just get to our horizon and see what's after it because whatever it is it's got to be better than this right? Right? Right? So let's just go. Let's just go now –

A year passes through **Kate**, *and the horizon starts to pull itself away from the earth.*

Kate   Let's just –

Let's – Are you still –

Are you listening to me still?

Are you – Can you –

Another year passes through **Kate**.

Kate   Can you – There's – Can you –

Another year passes through **Kate**.

Kate   Can you hear that?

Another year passes through **Kate**.

Kate   Can you hear that happening? Are you still –

Another year passes through **Kate**.

Kate   It's – Are you still here and can you –

Another year passes through **Kate**.

Kate   Can you hear that happening to me?

Another year passes through **Kate**.

Kate   Can you hear time –

Another year passes through **Kate**.

Kate   Can you hear time crashing through me?

Another year passes through **Kate**.

Kate   Can you hear that?

Another year passes through **Kate**.

Kate   Can you – Can you hear all that time crashing and ripping through me?

Another year passes through **Kate** *and the horizon stops moving away.*

Kate   And can you see that? In between the earth and the sky. The horizon. It's just a space with nothing inside of it.

Three

Dave   Fuck you doing here?

Long pause.

Kate   Just ended up here.

Pause.

Dave   Taking yourself out for a drink or something?

Kate   No.

Dave   No?

Kate   Don't drink.

Dave   Bollocks don't you.

Kate   I don't. Not touched a drop since.

Dave   Right.

Pause.

You look terrible.

Kate   Older. Aren't I?

Dave   Don't look older much. Just look terrible.

They look at each other for a moment. **Kate** *looks away.*

Kate   You look –

Long pause.

Kate   Steve in there?

Dave   Who?

Kate   Bloke with the one eye?

Dave   One-eye Steve?

Kate *nods.*

Dave   Why'd you want him?

Kate   I don't.

Beat.

Just. Making conversation.

They look at each other for a moment. **Kate** *looks away.*

Dave   Tell you something you've got some balls haven't you?

Kate   Why's that?

Dave   Coming up here? Knew I drank here didn't you?

They look at each other for a moment. **Kate** *looks away.*

Kate   Bit of a surprise?

. . .

Alex   No.

Kate   Is to me a bit.

Alex   Why's that then?

Kate   Just thought something would have changed. Nothing has though. Town looks. Looks the same.

They look at each other for a moment. **Kate** *looks away.*

Alex   Did you want something? Most people just buy what they want then leave you know? Sort of how shopping works isn't it?

Kate   Looking for a job.

Alex   Really?

Kate   Guess so.

Alex   Right well can't help you with that.

Kate   Sign in the window says you're needing people.

Alex   We're not.

Pause.

Kate   OK.

They look at each other for a moment. **Kate** *looks away.*

Can I ask you something?

Alex   What?

Kate   Are you –

Beat.

Are you pretending?

. . .

Dave   What?

Kate   Said is it a bit of a surprise or something.

Dave   What seeing you?

Kate   Yeah.

Dave   No.

Kate   Why not?

Dave   Knew you were about. Saw you walking down the ring road. Looked like a ghost.

Pause.

Dave   When'd you get out?

Kate   Today. Got here this morning.

They look at each other for a moment. **Kate** *looks away.*

Dave   Back at your old house then?

Kate   Yeah.

Dave   Bit empty is it?

Pause. **Kate** *nods a little.*

Dave   Guess that's alright though. Don't have to listen to your dad dying any more. Not that you gave much of a shit before anyway.

They look at each other for a moment. **Kate** *looks away.*

Kate   Want me to leave?

Dave   Do what you like doesn't bother me.

Kate   Why not?

Dave   Because you're a waste of fucking air that's why.

. . .

Alex   Am I pretending?

Kate   Yeah.

Alex   Am I pretending what?

Kate   To not know who I am?

Alex   No.

They look at each other for a moment. **Kate** *looks away.*

Kate   Been away a long time haven't I?

Alex   Guess so.

Kate   Eleven years.

Pause.

Eleven years spinning inside my head.

They look at each other for a moment. **Kate** *looks away.*

You – Are you –

Beat.

Kate   You sell that extra-strong cider?

Alex   Yeah.

Kate   I'll have some of that.

Alex   If you've got the money.

Kate   I'll owe you.

Alex   Can't do that.

Kate   Need something to stop my head spinning you know? And I – I just –

They look at each other for a moment. **Kate** *looks away.*

Kate   Don't give me any. Ignore me. Just ignore me.

Alex   Couldn't give you any anyway.

Kate   Yeah I know but I know myself and I think you know what I'm like too so I feel like I could just nick it from you anyway and when you go to stop me I'll just explode. But I shouldn't be asking. Because I've not drank since. And I'm – I've. I've been sober for a while now but it's just your eyes.

When I look at your eyes and skin and hair and the way you stand you look just like her.

It's like I'm talking to a ghost.

. . .

Dave   Aren't you? Waste of air.

Kate   Yeah?

Dave   Yeah. Waste of air. Scum.

Kate   Came to say sorry.

Dave   What for?

Kate   For what I did. I'm sorry.

Dave   Alright.

Kate   That it?

Dave   That it what?

Kate   Just alright and that's it?

Dave   Dunno what more you want. Was ages ago. Most people have forgotten about it. Got on with life. No one's been waiting for a piece of shit like you.

Kate   Piece of shit?

Dave   What?

Kate   That what I am?

Dave   Course you are.

Kate   What else am I?

Dave   What?

Kate   Scum? That it? You've always thought that about me haven't you? What else am I?

Dave   Oh I get it.

Kate   What?

Dave   I know what you're after.

Kate   What's that?

Dave   You're trying to wind me up. Just like you used to. Throwing up on my car. Licking booze off my drive. Waking up my kid. Trying to wind me up like you used to when you came knocking for my brother. I know what you want.

Kate   What do I want?

Dave   For me to smack you. I know. But I'm not going to do that. I'm not going to do that.

Kate   Know you want to.

Dave   Do you now?

Kate   I think you do. I think you should and all. Smash a fist into my mouth. Knock a few teeth out. Make me bleed. I think you want to do that to me because of what I did.

Dave   Nah I'm not going to do that.

Kate   Why?

Dave   Because you want me to do that because you want to feel something. And I'm not going to give you that.

Kate   Why not?

Dave   Don't deserve it.

Kate   What do I deserve then?

Dave looks at **Kate** *a moment. Smiles. Shakes his head.*

Dave   What you've got now.

Kate   Which is what?

. . .

Alex   You're not though are you?

Kate   What?

Alex   You're not talking to a ghost. Because I'm not her. I'm me. And I'm alive. And she's dead. Because you killed her in a car crash because you were drunk and fucked off your head on drugs.

Pause. **Kate** *closes her eyes for a moment. Opens them.*

Kate   I know I just –

They look at each other for a moment. **Kate** *looks away.*

Kate   Do you hate me?

Alex   No.

Kate   Why not?

Alex   Don't care about you enough to hate you.

Kate   What do you think of me then?

Alex   Don't think anything of you. Don't think anyone should think anything of you.

Long pause.

Kate   She used to carry you about in a sports bag. Packed it with soft stuff. Made you comfy. Wanted to keep you safe. Didn't want you to hear your parents shouting at each other. You remember that?

Alex   No.

Pause. **Kate** *nods. Can't look anywhere but at her feet. She is tense.*

Kate   She did. Why don't you remember that?

Alex   Because I don't.

Kate   I do. I remember it. I remember it all. That's all I do. Just remember it all. My head. Just goes round and round. Spins around them both.

They look at each other for a moment. **Kate** *looks away.*

Kate   I think I need you to say you hate me. Would you do that for me?

Alex   No.

Kate   Why not?

Alex   Because I'm not going to give you anything that you want.

Kate   Do you forgive me?

Alex   No.

Kate   So you do hate me then?

Alex   No.

Kate   Then what?

Alex   I feel nothing for you. That's all. Not going to help you. You know? Not going to do that for you.

. . .

Dave   Whatever's inside that messed-up car crash of a mind. Whatever's spinning around there. That's what you deserve. To be constantly haunted by the ghost of my brother and the other one you killed. What was her name?

Beat.

Kate   Sam.

Dave   Sam that's it. Samantha. Sister works in the shop doesn't she? Looks just like her. Quite funny really.

Kate   What is?

Dave   All this. You coming back here walking around. Looking for a fight. Or something to make you feel something that isn't just wanting. Think it's quite funny. Can keep trying to wind me up. Not going to hit you. Have another go if you like. Wind me up. Go on.

Beat.

Kate   Pete wanted to run away with your boy.

Dave   Oh yeah? Why'd he want to do that then?

Kate   Because he hated you.

Dave   Hated him and all. Streak of piss he was. Useless excuse for a person. Good thing you killed him really because it got him out the house and freed up some space. Want to try again?

Pause. **Kate** *looks at* **Dave**. *They stare at each other a bit.*

Kate   Where does that come from?

Dave   What?

Kate   That. That anger. That emptiness inside of you. Inside of us all. Inside of me.

Dave   What you going on about?

Kate   Is it just here? Is it in the bricks of towns like this? In the cracks of the roads and pavements? In the rust of closed shop signs? In the weeds growing out of ruined pubs? Is that where it is? Grows out of all that and gets into our heads? Because it's in you isn't it? And me. And all I wanted to do was run away from it. And take them away from it too. But I messed up. That's all. I didn't mean to do what I did. I was stupid. I know that. I do. But now this. Now this emptiness is all I have. And I don't want to feel that any more. I don't want to feel empty. So just hit me.

Dave   No.

Kate   He hated you. Hit me.

Dave   Keep trying all you like.

Kate   He hated you. He did. Hit me.

Dave   No.

Kate   Then just –

Just –

. . .

Kate   Just say you hate me.

Alex   No.

Kate   Please.

Alex   Are you begging?

Kate   No I'm just –

I'm just –

I'm –

I'm just.

Tired.

And

Kate *shuts her eyes tightly. She keeps her eyes closed.*

And I don't know how to make my head stop spinning. That's all it does. Because of what I've done. Spins around them. Them and all those little hopes inside their heads. Pete with his family. Sam with her flat. Those simple hopes. Where are they now? Can you tell me that? Are they still hanging in the air by the road where they died? Those tiny hopes that spill out of your head. All because of me. Because I was scared of being alone. Because I couldn't look after my dad. And wasn't brave enough to do that. Those hopes. Where –

Where do they go?

Kate *opens her eyes. She is very close to tears but holding them back. She tries to look at* **Alex***.*

Kate   How'd you do it? How'd you put yourself back together? Because I don't know how to do that.

You look just like her. So does he. It's like I'm being haunted by them. It's like I'm just walking round and round next to the ghosts inside my head. How'd you put yourself back together? When the pieces of yourself are just scattered about inside of your own head? I wish someone would tell me how to do that. I keep doing this. Going round and round. And it's always the same. And no one will tell me how to make it stop.

It's strange isn't it? How you think something will go the way you think. And then one moment. Just one. One moment out of every moment that exists in the whole universe happens to you and then it's gone. And now I just circle around that one moment. And it won't let me go.

Kate *looks at* **Alex***. Then away. The tears are just behind her eyes.*

Kate   How'd you put yourself back together? This time can you tell me?

Pause.

Alex I have to close the shop. So can you please get out.

Kate *looks down. Closes her eyes tight. And keeps them shut.*

Four

Will   Who you then? Never seen you about. Mad you're sitting in a playground on your own middle of the night. Nearly shit myself seeing you here. Thought you were a ghost. Nearly shit my pants. Glad I didn't. Always thought I would do that if I saw a ghost. Just see one and just be like I've shit myself. Then fall over. But you're not. Are you?

Kate *opens her eyes.*

Kate   What?

Will Just asking if you were a ghost and that? Please tell me you're not because I know I was joking about shitting myself before but if you were a proper ghost it wouldn't be a joke and I would literally just shit myself which is something I don't want.

Kate No I'm not.

Will That's a relief then because I hate shitting myself. Not that I do it ever. Just to be clear.

Liv Ignore him he's broken. What you doing here? Swings are all rusted. Don't work.

Kate Grew up here.

Liv Did you? Not seen you about.

Kate Been away for a while.

Will What you doing back here then? I wouldn't come back here if I left. Shithole.

Kate Nowhere else to be.

Will Loads of other places to be aren't there? Your age and all. Go anywhere. Go to the sea mate. That'd be quality. Go to the sea. Have a paddle. Be top that. Can't wait for a paddle about in the sea man. Can't beat that can you?

Liv What's your name?

Kate What?

Liv What's. Your. Name? Not a hard question is it mate.

Beat.

Kate Kate.

Liv Kate?

Will Just sitting here on your own then Kate?

Beat.

Kate Didn't know where else to go.

Will   Go to the pub? Old enough right?

Liv   Don't go to the Oak though because it's full of twats. Absolute twat cave that place. Where you been then?

Kate   What?

Liv   Said you came back? Assume you've been somewhere to come back?

Beat.

Kate   Prison.

Will   Prison?

Kate *nods.*

Will   Oh yeah why?

Kate   Just because.

Will   Just because? Don't go to prison just because do you? Have to have done something right?

Beat.

Kate   I killed my best friends in a car crash.

Will   Oh yeah?

Beat.

Well. That's not fun. You alright?

Beat.

Kate   What?

Will   Asked if you were alright. Proper sad that. You miss them?

Kate *nods.*

Liv   Were you drink driving or something?

Kate *nods.*

Liv   Yeah unlucky. What's that thing people say? Five and drive? Think it happens every year in our school. Just hear about that. Few kids die in a car crash. And then they're gone. Sad that. Still though. Everyone gets pissed and drives out here don't they. Towns like this. Not much else going on except look at a horizon that feels too far away. Shame really. Because they just need a bit of attention I guess. Like all of us sometimes. But what else is there to do hey? That where you got that scar from on your face?

Liv *reaches out and touches the scar on* **Kate***'s face.* **Kate** *just looks into* **Liv***'s eyes. They stare at each other for a bit.*

Kate   No.

Liv   Where's it from then?

Pause.

Kate   My mate. I made her punch me.

Will   Did you? That's funny.

Kate *nods.*

Kate   I think it's my favourite part of me.

Beat.

Liv   Is she dead?

Kate *nods.* **Liv** *drops her hand away.* **Will** *and* **Liv** *look at each other. There is a pause.*

Liv   Want to tell us?

Kate   What about?

Liv   About it all? Sitting in a playground on your own at night and all that. Don't look much fun. I mean we're only fifteen. Don't mind listening. And we're bored so nothing else to do.

Kate   You want me to tell you?

Will   Dunno. If you want to. I was going to tell her a story about how I got off with my mate's nan but yours sounds more interesting.

Beat.

Kate   Don't think you want to hear about it.

Liv   Might as well. We don't mind. Why wouldn't we want to hear?

Kate   Because.

Liv   Because why?

Long pause.

Kate   Because I don't think you'll care about me at the end. If I tell you what I've done. I don't think you'll care about me. Or like me. But standing here. Standing in front of you. In this dead town that I grew up in. I can't think about anything else. It all just circles round the inside of my head. And won't let me go. So maybe if I tell you it will. Maybe if I say it all out loud again it'll let me go. So I think I'll do that.

You probably won't like me. But maybe you will. I won't mind either way.

I just want it to let me go.

Because then.

Because then maybe I'll –

I'll be able to start again.

Five

Pete   Where from?

End.

Acknowledgements

Island Town wouldn't have been anything at all without the help, love and support of the following:

Stef O'Driscoll for all the notes and positivity and for pushing the play way beyond what I could have done on my own; Katherine Pearce, Jack Wilkinson and Charlotte O'Leary for filling it with sparks; Caitlin O'Reilly, Jennifer Jackson, Simon Carroll-Jones, Peter Small, Dominic Kennedy and Balisha Karra for helping to make it move and breathe; George Perrin and James Grieve for the belief in this and me; Everyone at Paines Plough for the constant support, love and all the rest; Harriet Pennington Legh and Becca Kinder, as always; Dom O'Hanlon; Georgia Christou and Vinay Patel, for all the guidance and support; and Mum, Dad and Phil, especially with this one.

Thank you.

Simon Longman

Methuen Drama Modern Plays

include work by

Bola Agbaje	Robert Holman
Edward Albee	Caroline Horton
Davey Anderson	Terry Johnson
Jean Anouilh	Sarah Kane
John Arden	Barrie Keeffe
Peter Barnes	Doug Lucie
Sebastian Barry	Anders Lustgarten
Alistair Beaton	David Mamet
Brendan Behan	Patrick Marber
Edward Bond	Martin McDonagh
William Boyd	Arthur Miller
Bertolt Brecht	D. C. Moore
Howard Brenton	Tom Murphy
Amelia Bullmore	Phyllis Nagy
Anthony Burgess	Anthony Neilson
Leo Butler	Peter Nichols
Jim Cartwright	Joe Orton
Lolita Chakrabarti	Joe Penhall
Caryl Churchill	Luigi Pirandello
Lucinda Coxon	Stephen Poliakoff
Curious Directive	Lucy Prebble
Nick Darke	Peter Quilter
Shelagh Delaney	Mark Ravenhill
Ishy Din	Philip Ridley
Claire Dowie	Willy Russell
David Edgar	Jean-Paul Sartre
David Eldridge	Sam Shepard
Dario Fo	Martin Sherman
Michael Frayn	Wole Soyinka
John Godber	Simon Stephens
Paul Godfrey	Peter Straughan
James Graham	Kate Tempest
David Greig	Theatre Workshop
John Guare	Judy Upton
Mark Haddon	Timberlake Wertenbaker
Peter Handke	Roy Williams
David Harrower	Snoo Wilson
Jonathan Harvey	Frances Ya-Chu Cowhig

Methuen Drama Contemporary Dramatists

include

John Arden (two volumes)
Arden & D'Arcy
Peter Barnes (three volumes)
Sebastian Barry
Mike Bartlett
Dermot Bolger
Edward Bond (ten volumes)
Howard Brenton (two volumes)
Leo Butler (two volumes)
Richard Cameron
Jim Cartwright
Caryl Churchill (two volumes)
Complicite
Sarah Daniels (two volumes)
Nick Darke
David Edgar (three volumes)
David Eldridge (two volumes)
Ben Elton
Per Olov Enquist
Dario Fo (two volumes)
Michael Frayn (four volumes)
John Godber (four volumes)
Paul Godfrey
James Graham (two volumes)
David Greig
John Guare
Lee Hall (two volumes)
Katori Hall
Peter Handke
Jonathan Harvey (two volumes)
Iain Heggie
Israel Horovitz
Declan Hughes
Terry Johnson (three volumes)
Sarah Kane
Barrie Keeffe
Bernard-Marie Koltès (two volumes)
Franz Xaver Kroetz
Kwame Kwei-Armah
David Lan
Bryony Lavery
Deborah Levy
Doug Lucie

David Mamet (four volumes)
Patrick Marber
Martin McDonagh
Duncan McLean
David Mercer (two volumes)
Anthony Minghella (two volumes)
Tom Murphy (six volumes)
Phyllis Nagy
Anthony Neilson (two volumes)
Peter Nichol (two volumes)
Philip Osment
Gary Owen
Louise Page
Stewart Parker (two volumes)
Joe Penhall (two volumes)
Stephen Poliakoff (three volumes)
David Rabe (two volumes)
Mark Ravenhill (three volumes)
Christina Reid
Philip Ridley (two volumes)
Willy Russell
Eric-Emmanuel Schmitt
Ntozake Shange
Sam Shepard (two volumes)
Martin Sherman (two volumes)
Christopher Shinn (two volumes)
Joshua Sobel
Wole Soyinka (two volumes)
Simon Stephens (three volumes)
Shelagh Stephenson
David Storey (three volumes)
C. P. Taylor
Sue Townsend
Judy Upton
Michel Vinaver (two volumes)
Arnold Wesker (two volumes)
Peter Whelan
Michael Wilcox
Roy Williams (four volumes)
David Williamson
Snoo Wilson (two volumes)
David Wood (two volumes)
Victoria Wood

For a complete listing of
Methuen Drama titles, visit:
www.bloomsbury.com/drama

Follow us on Twitter and keep up to date
with our news and publications
@MethuenDrama

Printed in the USA
CPSIA information can be obtained
at www.ICGtesting.com
LVHW020848171024
794056LV00002B/459